SO-BDP-052

Man, Woman and Priesthood

James Tolhurst (editor)
Graham Leonard
Mary Kenny
Andrew McGowan
Roman Cholij
J I Packer
and
Joyce Little

★

Leominster Bloomington

Gracewing.

First published in 1989 by

Gracewing
Fowler Wright Books
Burgess Street Leominster
Herefordshire HR6 8DE

Fowler Wright Books
Meyerstone Inc
2014 South Yoso Ave
Bloomington
Indiana 47403 USA

All rights reserved. No part of this publication may be reproduced, stored in a retrieval system, or transmitted in any form, or by any means, electronic, mechanical, photocopying, recording or otherwise, without the written permission of the publisher.

Text © 1989 by James Tolhurst, Graham Leonard, Mary Kenny, Andrew McGowan, Roman Cholij, Joyce Little and J I Packer

ISBN 0 85244 162 2

Typesetting by Print Origination (NW) Limited, Formby, Liverpool
Printed and bound in Great Britain by Billings & Sons Ltd, Worcester

to Michael Bowen,
Archbishop of Southwark
Pastor Bonus atque Pater.

The authors and publishers would like to acknowledge the kindness of the following individuals and publishers in allowing us to reproduce from their works

CONTENTS

Notes on Contributors

Bishop Graham Leonard was Bishop of Truro from 1973 to 1981, and has been Bishop of London since 1981. He is Dean of the Chapels Royal and a Privy Councillor. He has contributed to *A Critique of Eucharistic Agreement* (SPCK 1975) and is the author of *Life in Christ* (Mowbray 1986) and *Faith for the Future* (Church House 1986) among other works.

Rev. James Tolhurst DD is Parish Priest of St Joseph's, St Mary Cray. He has been involved in training students for the Permanent Diaconate and has contributed to many newspapers and magazines. His book on the Sermons of John Henry Newman, *The Church . . . A Communion* was published by Gracewing in 1988.

Rev. Andrew McGowan BD STM is a Church of Scotland minister in Bishopbriggs. He contributed articles to the *New Dictionary of Theology* (Inter Varsity Press 1988) and is Editor of *Women Elders in the Kirk?* (Christian Focus 1990).

Mary Kenny Lives in London and is married with two sons. She is a columnist for the *Sunday Telegraph* as well as a lecturer and broadcaster. Her books include *Why Christianity Works* (Michael Joseph 1981) and *Abortion: The Whole Story* (Quartet 1979).

Rev. Roman Cholij BSc JCD is the Private Secretary to the Apostolic Exarch for Ukrainians in Great Britain and Vice Chancellor. He has contributed to many periodicals and has just published *Clerical Celibacy in East and West* (Gracewing 1989).

Dr James I Packer MA DPhil is Professor of Historical and Systematic Theology at Regent College, Vancouver. He is author of *Knowing God* (Hodder & Stoughton 1975) and *Laid-back Religion* (Inter Varsity Press 1989) as well as numerous other titles.

Dr Joyce A Little is Associate Professor of Theology, University of St Thomas, Houston. A contributor to numerous periodicals, she has lectured and broadcast on the role of women in society.

Introduction

J. I. Packer

In the following set of essays Roman Catholic, Orthodox, Anglican and Presbyterian theologians unite to maintain against active feminist and passive egalitarian opinion that women should not be made priests in the church of God. It was not to be expected that writers from these four traditions would be perfectly agreed on every detail that they discuss, nor are they; but just as all feminists of whatever stripe think that it is wrong in principle to bar women from any office currently held by men, so these essayists agree that to set women to fulfil the liturgical, didactic, and governmental roles that the presbyteral and episcopal offices have historically involved is a wrong turning for the church in this or any age to take. That is the conviction on which they all converge.

On this question world Christendom is sharply divided: there is no secret about that! Great sections of the church (Baptist, Congregational, Lutheran, Methodist, and the currently exploding Pentecostal denominations; major Presbyterian bodies; leading Anglican provinces) have settled the issue on the practical level: with a variety of understandings of ordination, they are already commissioning women to fulfil these particular roles, and God, who is rich in mercy, blesses these women's ministry. Does not that prove the rightness of what has been done? Not necessarily; God has blessed his people before through intrinsically inappropriate arrangements, and might be doing the same again. The kindness of God in practice does not resolve questions of principle. In the Church of England, where at present women may only be ordained deacon, the latest poll gives 78% of the membership as favouring women priests: does not the size of the majority (assuming the poll is accurate) indicate the mind and will of God? Again, not necessarily. As Article 19 affirms that the churches of Jerusalem, Alexandria, Antioch and Rome have erred in matters of faith and obedience, so Anglican churches may themselves err through mistaken notions becoming majority opinions. And in the Roman Catholic Church itself, though the hierarchy speaks vigorously against women priests and bishops, the ground-swell of contrary opinion among theologians and lay people appears in some quarters to grow stronger by the hour. To the authors of this book, however, it seems clear that the prevalence of the positions they oppose is due to secular social and pragmatic pressures rather than to any propriety of principle, and they hope that their own principled approach will contribute to showing this. Meantime, they remember Jeremiah and Athanasius, and retain confidence in their cause.

Let it be emphatically said, however, that what this book opposes is not the ministry of women. The writers must not be accused of doubting that women have as significant a place as men in the every-member ministry pattern that is God's plan for all congregations; nor must they be supposed to want to turn the clock back and confine women to narrow domestic roles, or to exclude them from careers of service in salaried employment on church and denominational staffs. Each of these writers, like myself, will affirm the gifts of God to women, and rejoice in them, and venture the view that the church does not as yet make anything like as much of women's ministry as it should. All that is being argued is that presbyteral and episcopal ministry, as such, should be for men only in the future, just as it has been in most of the Christian church for most of the Christian past. The reasons for this restriction are biblical and theological: they have to do with a shared understanding – indeed, a shared vision – of key realities in Christianity, as such. This the reader will soon see.

The writers are moved by some or all of the following five arguments.

(1) The argument from *the authority of Scripture*.

It is often said that the Bible is the book of the church, that the church antedoted all apostolic writings, and that the church gave us the Bible, by identifying the canonical New Testament that should be set alongside the Jewish Scriptures to form the Christian rule of faith and life. Those statements are true, but they belong with a further set of statements, thus: (i) all Scripture is in its own nature divine witness and instruction, teaching from God given in the form of teaching from men; (ii) apostolic testimony to Christ, oral and written, is integral to the fact of Christ, inasmuch as Christ himself poured out the Spirit on the apostles to enable them to witness to him truly; (iii) the assumption of those who identified the New Testament canon was that God created it, by inspiring the books that make it up, and the church's part is just to recognize and receive it as God's gift; (iv) the Bible, and the New Testament in particular, is a God-given guide and control for the church's faith, the divine authority of which the church must acknowledge. When Roman Catholics and Orthodox insist that their tradition is verifiable from Scripture, and when Anglicans and Presbyterians affirm that Scripture must ever stand in a critical, corrective, constitutive and creative relation to the church's faith, all four are agreeing that Bible teaching has divine authority, and the church may not sit loose to God's instruction in the written Word. For the writers of this book, this is undisputed common ground.

Now, it is certainly true that Scripture celebrates in all sorts of ways the dignity and glory of womanhood, and that the Gospels highlight Jesus' affirmation of particular women as disciples and friends, and that ministering women often appear in the narrative of Acts and in the letters of Paul. But it is also true that Scripture knows nothing of women being chosen as apostles or presbyters, and that Paul places restrictions on the part that women may play in public worship in comparison with men (see 1 Cor. 11:2-16; 14:33-36; 1 Tim. 2:8-14). Whatever precisely these passages are taken to mean (and the exegetical problems that they present are notorious), they are certainly restrictive, in a way that on any exegesis would make apostolic or presbyteral ministry for a woman of Paul's day impossible. Granted, hypotheses have been formed that would make the restrictions inapplicable to Christian women today; these are educated guesses about what Paul would say were he alive now. But they are only guesses, after all; they involve special pleading, and inevitably fall short of certainty; they are far too hazardous to serve as a basis for revamping historic church order. All we can be sure of is that Paul used his apostolic authority to restrict women's leading in worship in a way that made presbyteral ministry impossible for them; that he based this restriction on the events of the creation and the fall (1 Tim. 2:12-14), which he saw as disclosing universal truth about the two sexes together; and that the guess that he would rescind the restriction were he alive today is no more than a guess - in other words, a speculation, incapable of proof.

What should we make of these facts? Those for whom Bible teaching is spotty human speculation about God throughout, rather than infallible wisdom from God himself, and who want to see the church bring itself up-to-date by climbing on to secular band wagons, will brush them off as being hopelessly out of line with modern attitudes. But for the writers of this book the only safe, unitive, and God-honouring way is to retain the Pauline restrictions – as Paul himself, were he back with us today, might very well direct us to do.

(2) The argument from *the knowledge of Christ*.

That the essence of Christianity is the knowledge of Jesus Christ the Lord, the incarnate Son of God, as the royal messenger and high priest as in Hebrews, as the head, husband, and cornerstone of the church that is his body, bride, and building as in Ephesians, and as the lamb and lifegiver portrayed in John's gospel – to look no further – is the veriest truism. That is not to deny that it is a truth needing constant reassertion, but simply to categorize it as a truth that no one who takes the slightest interest in Christianity should be able to miss, since it is basic to the New Testament. Though Christ is there presented and explained in many ways (all consistent with each other and forming a coherent whole, be it said – the contrary view, though fashionable among academics, is exegetically myopic), the apostolic writers are unanimous in their belief that Christianity is in essence faith-knowledge of Jesus. They are unanimous too as to what this involves: knowing Christ for them has a relational and affectional, as well as an intellectual dimension; they see knowledge of the Saviour as a matter of cognition and communion, trust and obedience, love and adoration, all combined. To know Christ, on their view, is to worship him, to work for him, and to walk with him; it is to repent before him, to rely upon him, and to rejoice in him; it is peace, joy, and contentment; it is salvation; it is heaven on earth.

Nor is this all. We are redeemed, as we were created, for community, and the new life that Christ gives us individually, so we learn, is meant to be lived out corporately, in the body-life of mutual ministry and the liturgical life of united worship that together constitute the true existence of the church. In all ministry, from the informal spontaneities of every-member fellowship to the preaching, teaching, sacramental actions, and disciplinary pastoral care carried out by stated leaders, officially commissioned in the historic orders, Christ himself is the true minister, giving himself and his gifts to his needy people as they hear and share his word. That Christ is always the real minister is the deepest of all truths about ministry, yet it is one that is constantly forgotten, or at least disregarded. So what to do? The rational course is not far to seek. All structures of ministry in the church should be so designed as to create and sustain with maximum force faith-knowledge that it is Christ himself, Jesus of Nazareth risen and glorified, who ministers to us, communicating knowledge of his grace and goodness, his power and purpose, his will, work, and ways, making vivid to us his own reality, and drawing us deeper into his love for the Father and for the world; and doing all this through the words and acts of his ministering servants, who are his medium of ministry to us here and now.

This is the basis for the second argument, which in its simplest form is as follows: Since the Son of God was incarnate as a human male, it will always be easier, other things being equal, to realise and remember that Christ in person is ministering when his human agent and representative is also male. Some will stiffen this argument by appeal to the iconic principle that bulks large in Orthodox devotion, and by affirming, as both Roman Catholics and Orthodox do, that the ordained minister (male) shares in Christ's high priesthood in a specially close way. Protestants may demur at both notions, but on the common-sense principle that a male is best represented by another male there ought to be agreement; just as there should be in rejecting the thought that Jesus should be imaged as androgynous, or at any rate that imaging his maleness is not important. For Jesus was not, and is not, merely a symbol of something, or a source of teaching that can stand on its own without reference to the teacher. On the contrary, Jesus is the second man, the last Adam, our great high priest and sacrifice, our prophet, priest, and king (not prophetess, priestess, and queen), and he is all this precisely in his maleness. To minimize the maleness shows a degree of failure to grasp the space-time reality and redemptive significance of the incarnation. The proper conclusion to draw, therefore, without in the least denying that informally Christ ministers through women no less than through men, is that it is regularly better and more edifying that Jesus' official representatives in the church's ongoing life should be male.

(3) The argument from *the understanding of humanness*. The contention here is easy to state. God made humanity in two genders. Human males and females both bear his image and in personal dignity are equal in every way. But God set them in a non-reversible relation to each other, which finds expression both in the story of Eve being made from the man's rib, to be a help to him (Gen. 2:20-23), and in Paul's assertion of male headship, not simply in marriage (Eph. 5:23), but in the human race as such (1 Cor. 11:3, 11 f.). The creation pattern, like the marriage pattern (which is in fact the creation pattern applied to the peak-relation between the sexes - nothing more, nothing less), may therefore be summarized thus: man to lead, woman to support; man to initiate, woman to enable; man to take responsibility for the well-being of women, women to take responsibility for helping men. Should these relational dynamics be disregarded (as today, of course, in pagan and post-Christian cultures they often are), strains are put on the nature of both men and women,

the full self-discovery and fulfilment that God meant men and women to find in cooperation together will be missed, and some of the respect due to our wise Creator will perish. But bishops and presbyters are ordained to a role of authoritative pastoral leadership; and such a role is for masculine men rather than womanly women, according to the creation pattern which redemption aims to restore.

(4) The argument from *the character of the church*.

Probably the deepest division in Christendom today is over the question of what the church on earth is called to be - a question involving not only theological analysis, but imaginative vision too. For Roman Catholics and Orthodox, the church is essentially worshippers united with clergy in a supernatural sacramental institution, called to stand as God's bulwark amid the tossing waves of restless human folly. For Protestants of Reformational type, the church is essentially believers receiving instruction and encouragement from God through the Bible and the Lord's Supper, learning thereby to sanctify the secular and Christianize the local culture. For Protestant liberals (the dominant type of Protestant for the past century) and for pietistic evangelical groupings that focus on experience (there are many such), the church is essentially a service organisation for various kinds of care and outreach. Churchpeople of the first and second type believe strongly in revealed truth and see faithful guardianship of it as integral to the church's calling; churchpeople of the third type believe in revealed truth weakly or not at all, and the liberals among them are explicit that sympathetic identification with the aspirations and felt needs of the current culture is much nearer the heart of the Christian vocation than detachment from dominant thought patterns can ever be. Adherents of the first two understandings of the church look for the Holy Spirit to guide God's people from the Bible and the church's own heritage of wisdom; adherents of the third position envisage the Holy Spirit making his mind known through external pressures that suggest to the church ways of serving the world more comprehensively. For the first two of these types, stability is continually with the proven wisdom of the Christian past is the sure path of greatest usefulness in the present, while for the third willingness to change radically in order to keep in step with secular developments of whatever kind is one of the church's prime virtues, a litmus test of genuine willingness to serve. The dictum that the world must write the agenda for the church crystallizes this conviction, and the taking up within the church of the feminist insistence that all offices held by men should be open to women too is an example of its outworking.

At this point there is no meeting of minds, for there is no shared vision. Those whose church-consciousness bears the shape of the first or second mould see the third way of believing in the church as an undermining and betraying of authentic Christian supernaturalism all along the line, and certainly so in the matter of ordaining women bishops and priests. In their minds, the three arguments that we have reviewed already – that the New Testament does not envisage or encourage this course, and arguably forbids it; that women priests and bishops will hinder rather than help forward awareness of the reality of Christ's ministry through his ministers; and that these offices require personal qualities that women generically are not fitted by their Creator to provide – combining with the thought that the church is under no compulsion to conform to the world, but has indeed been warned against doing that, to form a fourth consideration counselling against the proposed course of action.

There are here two contradictory visions of the church's calling, the first requiring its adherents to negate and bale out from the church the fashionable secularities which the second vision prompts its adherents to pour in. This dissonance of vision, which currently appears in nearly all churches and denominations, is a tragically weakening thing; which vision is authentic, and which mistaken (for they cannot both be right) is a matter that calls for further urgent discussion. But that is more than can be undertaken here.

(5) The argument from *the example of Mary*.

The relevance of what we know of Jesus' mother to this discussion will be differently assessed by different people; but those who see Mary as the supreme model of devotion and discipleship for all God's children, and doubly so for his women, may properly point to her as final proof of the non-necessity of ordination for a woman who wishes to serve the Father and the Son, and of the possibility of rendering incalculably significant service in unordained roles and informal ministries.

The debate about the priesthood so widely canvassed for women must and will continue; it is not over yet, and theologically, as distinct from pragmatically and administratively, it may hardly have begun. The essays and official materials contained in this book will at least help to clarify, theologically, what is at stake. May God unite his people in his truth and in the procedures that accord with it, in this as in all the disputes that divide us today. Truly, our hope is in him.

The Priesthood of Christ

Graham Leonard

"Being taken from among men, is appointed for men in things pertaining unto God"

These words from the opening verse of Chapter V of the Epistle to the Hebrews, while referring to the high priesthood of Christ, might well be used to describe the institution of priesthood as it has been found in human history. Priesthood in one form or another has been a force in the social structure of the community as a means by which human beings seek to relate their awareness of a transcendental power, whether conceived of as benevolent or hostile, to the circumstances of life and the needs of the community. It is to be found in history in many diverse forms but such is its fundamental purpose. As Karl Rahner has said, "Priesthood belongs to the normal, enduring institutions of human life" and he points out that "sacrifice (that is, priestly activity) could originally be carried out by every accepted authority in human society (patriarch head of a family, chief of a clan, prince) and the priesthood, being organised on a social and even caste basis, could be bequeathed in a fixed order and handed down without diminution".[1] St Augustine's definition of true sacrifice as "every action which is performed with the aim of inhering God in one holy society; whose purpose, that is, is to bring us to the end by which we can truly be made blessed", reflects the universality of sacrifice, and thereby of priesthood, in expressing the fears and hopes of man.

But, as Martin D'Arcy points out in his classic work 'The Mind and Heart of Love', "Unfortunately, the true aim of sacrifice is often obscured by the primitive passions which deflect man's ideals and also by the intrusion of other motives. At one moment magic and superstition have usurped the place of religion; at another, the desire to make religion profitable and to exploit the invisible power of the gods. But there are the parasitical growths; they do not help to show us the main stems. In its purest, and therefore, most exemplary forms sacrifice is always homage and adoration, petition and request for pardon, and in the end the longing to be possessed by God and to possess Him".[2]

In modern secular society, when such awareness is reduced to a rudimentary degree, the need for such an institution still remains. Even the most secular thinkers appeal to some authority which is not merely personal to themselves but an authority which they expect and sometimes try to ensure that others will recognize and obey. Such an institution is necessary if the impulses, desires and emotions of human beings are to be ordered within the domestic, economic and political organizations of society for the good of all. When priesthood as conceived in the past in a religious context is denied, ignored or minimized, society tends to look for the role to be fulfilled by other symbolic figures such as philosophers and politicians in the eighteenth century, scientists in the nineteenth and sociologists and television personalities in the twentieth. Such are given an authority over and above what most of them would claim for themselves.

In Christ, priesthood, like any other human institution, is transformed, not destroyed or abolished. He who redeems the world is he by whom it was created. Redemption does not destroy that which was seen by God to be very good but liberates it from the corrupting and destructive effects of sin and so enables it to fulfil its true purpose.

In considering the role of priesthood today in the Church and thereby for the world, it is essential to begin with the high priesthood of Christ and to learn how the priesthood both of the ordained priesthood within the Church, and the priesthood of the whole Church derive from the priesthood of Christ and are related to it. But it is also essential to consider how the high priesthood of Christ is related to and how it fulfils priesthood and sacrifice as integral constituents of human life. It is fatally easy to conceive of priesthood in pre-Christian or pagan terms. The purpose of some forms of it was, and in parts of the world still is, to appease, manipulate or coerce a capricious or hostile god or gods. Other forms have sought to enable worshippers to lose themselves in the force of some overwhelming passion by inducing ecstacy. Such ideas are to be found within Christian Communities today.

The redemption and transformation of priesthood effected by Christ demanded a radical change in the understanding of man's relationship to God. It is the change summed up most succinctly in the words of St John, "Herein is love, not that we loved God but that he loved us".[3] Man does not have to seek to justify himself in the eyes of God, or seek to persuade God by one means or other to look favourably upon him. God who is love provides the sacrifice and bears the cost. Responding to the divine initiation and accepting the power of grace, man is enabled to offer himself in true and living sacrifice and to do so in the spirit of love. Such response and acceptance is not easy for man because of the self-centredness of sin, which makes him reject such dependence. It is significant that the philosophers of the Enlightenment, such as Feuerbach, rejected belief in God because they believed it to require a denial of the autonomy and authenticity of man.

The temptation to reject dependence remains, as does the failure to accept that dependence upon God, and to a lesser extent, upon one another, is the way to freedom and the affirmation of the true self. But in the present day, other powerful factors make it difficult for Christians to appreciate the true meaning of priesthood and sacrifice. As a result, priesthood is rejected or where the institution remains, is so modified that its power and effects are made to depend upon human attitudes instead of the promises and power of God.

The first such factor is to be found in the rejection of suffering as an integral element in human life if it is to be based on love. One deeply held belief in our society is that suffering is the worst evil and that anything, however morally wrong, is justified if it appears to relieve suffering. With it goes the corollary that men and women must have what they want without cost. Dorothy Soelle, in a passage which I have quoted elsewhere, writes eloquently of the kind of life which results, a life "with a corresponding disappearance of passion for life and of the strength and intensity of its joy". She writes, "I have in mind a society in which: a marriage that is perceived as unbearable ends in divorce; after divorce no scars remain; relationships between generations are dissolved as quickly as possible, without a struggle, without a trace; periods of mourning are 'sensibly' short; with haste the handicapped and sick are removed from the house and the dead from mind. If changing marriage partners happens as readily as trading in an old car for a new one, then the experiences that one had in the old relationship remain unproductive. From suffering nothing is learned and nothing is to be learned. In the equilibrium of a suffering free state the life curve flattens out so that even joy and happiness can no longer be experienced intensely. But more important than this consequence of apathy is the desensitization that freedom from suffering involves, the inability to perceive reality".[4]

The second factor is the habit of polarisation, by which qualities in human nature, which should be held in complementarity, are separated and seen in isolation. Either/or is the common cry, when it should be both/and. Examples of this commonly found are to be seen in individual fulfilment compared with the good of the community, the experiences of the body compared with life in the spirit or the creation of wealth and the welfare society. In the political sphere, again and again one party advocates a solution to a problem and does so rejecting one advocated by another, whereas the problem demands both solutions, which are not exclusive and which can check and control each other. In the sphere of priesthood and of any structure or order in the Church, the cultic and the personal are seen in opposition. A rightful concern for the cultic to be given its true interior significance and intention is often taken as a demand for the rejection of the active; with the result that subjective attitudes become the only criteria for determining the sacramental life of the Church and its ministry. The same separation of two elements which should be held in complementarity is to be found between sacramental grace and faith. Sacramental grace flows from the promises of God, who loves us to the end, even in our sins. At the same time, I do not think that any theologian has denied the need for faith on the part of the recipient if sacramental grace is to benefit the recipient and bear fruit in holiness of life. But in these days, such is the emphasis on faith that the very existence of the love of God towards us is made to depend upon it. So we read in the words of one contemporary Catholic theologian that "without the exercise of the faith no sacramental presence of Christ or the Passio Christi is possible".[5] Realising, it seems, that such a conclusion leads to a subjective attitude to the sacraments which makes the love of God conditional upon man's response, Fr. Kilmartin suggests that it is the faith of the Church rather than that of individuals which provides what is necessary. In one sense, this is true, but he precedes his consideration with these words "The tendency toward objectification of means of salvation in Western theology (and also Eastern theology) has led to an implicit, largely unreflective acceptance of the view that Christ somehow binds his presence to institutions which operate independently of the faith of the Church" and says that "the traditional institution placed on 'physical succession' of ordination going back to the apostles and on the institution of sacraments by Jesus during his earthly life by explicit or implicit words points in this direction and appears to be connected with the desire to secure not so much a more general Christology as an institutional basis for the sacraments which would guarantee Christ's presence over against the vicissitudes of the faith of the community". This argument leads him to a strange conclusion: "The presence of Christ is given as personal presence through the faith of the Church. Therefore, it obtains a certain objectivity. It is neither dependent on the faith of the minister nor on the faith of any particular community. But it is not independently linked to definite institutions or notions. The obedience of Christ is the way by which the Lordship of God was fully inserted into the world and the obedience of the faith of the Church is the way by which Christ remains personally present and effective in the Church." From this argument it is hard to avoid the conclusion that the presence and effectiveness of Christ is dependent upon this obedience. In so far as this is not constant, it is difficult to see what objectivity it gives to the Sacraments. It would seem that Fr. Kilmartin's at times rather tortuous arguments spring from a determination to make the operation of the Sacraments dependent upon the human response. Underlying them is, what to my mind is, a false assumption that the doctrine of ex

opere oper... a guarantee and
remove th... ...ne, while retain-
ing the n... are to be received
rightly, ...onal love of God,
which c... ...t or ignore him. A
similar ... ...rtin's consideration
of the ... ...ich he says, can be
used t... ...'ordained is claimed
perm... the Church". If the
orda... ...ental expression of the
con... ...ver his Church and his
tot... ...ning of the irrevocable
na... ...mes clear. In so far as a
pr... ...hat may, he witnesses to
t... ...ail his flock, though men
... ...irrevocable nature of the
... ...inder to all Christians that,
... ...ess of God, a Christian can
... ...an only become an apostate.
...s springing from the uncon-
... of God and the need for the
...n must be held together.
...common rejection of ontology
... functionalism. By that I mean
...ring what people and things *are*,
..., such consideration being re-
... which affirms that it is only what
people ...ters. In terms of the Christian life,
the distinction ... be put very simply. It is the
distinction between the Christian life as given by God, a
life which by grace we then seek to live out and to
implement, and the Christian life as understood in terms
of life which is constituted by the way we act, believe,
and feel. As Professor R H Fuller has written, "It is not
just a quirk of the Greek mind but a universal human
apperception that action implies prior being - even if, as
is also true, being is only apprehended in action".[6]

The rejection of the ontological has very profound effects. In the first place, it leads to an unwillingness to face reality and to accept what Gerard Manley Hopkins called the "is-ness" of things (and of ourselves). We adopt the attitude that things are what we want them to be, not what they are.

But secondly, it is essential to consider "being" before we consider 'action', if we are to understand the Christian Gospel. We are what we are as Christians by the sheer grace of God and by his creative and redeeming actions. We are not Christians because of what we have done or the way in which we have lived so that we have come to merit certain benefits from God. "By grace are ye saved through faith; and that not of yourselves; it is the gift of God".[7] It is by God's creative act that we are now creatures in Christ. So St Paul, in the majority of his letters, begins by praising God for what he has done and for what we are by grace and then, beginning with some such phrase as 'For this cause' or 'Wherefore', exhorts us to live out the meaning of what we are by grace.

The last factor affecting our approach to priesthood and reflecting contemporary thought which needs to be mentioned concerns the nature of the Sacraments. Such is the emphasis on the interior attitude which is necessary if the grace of the sacraments is to bear fruit, that their true nature and purpose is obscured and neglected. They are essentially sacraments of the New Covenant. They are, as the Articles of Religion of the Church of England affirm "not only badges or tokens of Christian men's profession but rather they be certain sure witnesses and effectual signs of grace by which he doth work invisibly in us, and doth not only quicken but also strengthen and confirm our Faith in him".[8] Article XXVI says they are effective because of Christ's institution and promise. For this reason the sacraments enable us to come to God in the words of the Prayer

Book Communion Service "not trusting in our own righteousness", but in the "manifold and great mercy" of God. Sacramental signification in this sense is peculiarly and uniquely Christian. It is made possible by the re-creation of the material universe effected in the body of Christ which he offered in total obedience upon the Cross, so liberating matters to be the instrument of divine grace.

With these considerations in mind we turn to the exposition of the high priesthood of Christ in the Epistle of the Hebrews, from which the ordained priesthood and the royal priesthood of the whole Church are derived and to which they are inextricably related.

The author of the Epistle expounds the meaning of the high priesthood of Christ by contrasting it with the priesthood and sacrificial systems of the Old Testament. Both have a distinctive character being based on the Old Covenant of God with his chosen people. Both developed considerably during Israel's history from the time of the patriarchs to that of the Temple in Jerusalem in the first Century B.C. but the principles underlying them are constant. Obedience to the Covenant required holiness, and the purpose of the various sacrifices was both to honour God as King, to cleanse the worshipper from impurity and to reaffirm on man's side the relationship given by God to his chosen people. The reality of sin as damaging that relationship was recognised as was the fact that the sacrifices commanded by the Law did not expiate for deliberate sin. This was made evident on the Day of Atonement when after two sin offerings, the one for the high priest and the other for the people, the priest laid his hands on a living goat and confessed the people's sins, transferring those sins to the goat which was then driven into the wilderness.

At the same time it was the work of the prophets to declare that holiness required moral as well as ceremonial purity, thereby developing awareness of the fact the sacrificial system did not expiate for sin. As is clear from the Dead Sea Scrolls, with their emphasis on the need for purity of heart and right interior intention, this process continued after the day of the great prophets up to the time of our Lord.

In Christ the work of both priest and prophet are fulfilled. "God, who at sundry times and in diverse manners spake in times past unto the fathers by the prophets, hath in these days spoken unto us by his Son".[9] The will of God is made known perfectly in the Word made flesh. The same Incarnate Word came to put away sin by the sacrifice of himself. Both in the manifestation of the will of God and in its obedience, he fulfils the role of priest and prophet.

The Epistle to the Hebrews begins with a strong affirmation of the uniqueness of the work of Christ and of the fact that in him, God himself has acted and still acts for the redemption of mankind. It is the "Son, whom he appointed heir to all things, through whom also he made the world, who being the effulgence of his glory and the very image of his substance and upholding all things by the word of his power, when he had made purification of sins, sat down on the right hand of the Majesty on high"[10]. It is the Son who tasted death to bring many sons unto glory and who was the author of their salvation.

To emphasize his point, the author uses seven texts from Scripture, which would have particular authority for his Jewish readers. The first three show that Christ is truly God's Son and far superior to any angels; the second three proclaim that he is the Creator who rules for ever, and in the seventh, he is proclaimed as the glorified Christ risen from the dead and seated at the right hand of the Father. In Chapter 3, while recognizing the work of Moses as the "mediator of the Old Covenant", the author tells us to look beyond Moses to Christ, who is the Apostle and High Priest.[11] He is the

Apostle because he is sent forth by the Father. He is also our High Priest because he offered sacrifice for the atonement of sin. So in his own person Our Lord fulfilled the work of Moses the lawgiver and his brother Aaron the Priest. Christ the Apostle gives us the Law like Moses but as the Incarnate Word of God. He is also our High Priest who offers sacrifice for us, and it is this fact which the author develops in Chapter 5.

There he shows how Christ fulfils the qualities which were required for a high priest of the Levitical Order. He lists four such qualities. First, he must be a member of the human race as his duty is to represent man before God. "For as much then as the children are partaking of flesh and blood, he also himself likewise took part of the same; that through death he might destroy him that had the power of death, that is, the devil".[12] Secondly, he is appointed by God "and does not take the honour unto himself"[13]. Thirdly, he is compassionate and shares the suffering of the people "Though he was a Son, yet learned obedience by the things which he suffered and having been made perfect, he became unto all those that obey him the author of eternal salvation"[14]. So he is named of God a high priest after the Order of Melchizedek. The introduction of this mysterious figure is to serve the author's purpose of showing that the priesthood of Christ, foreshadowed in the priesthood of Melchizedek, is greatly superior to the Levitical priesthood of the Old Testament. Melchizedek in Genesis XIV is a king and priest whose name means 'king of righteousness'. The name of his city, Salem, means 'peace' and the two qualities of righteousness and peace are associated with him. In the Genesis story, Melchizedek brings bread and wine to refresh Abraham and his companions after he had defeated the kings from the north. Melchizedek offered some of the bread and wine in sacrifice to the most High God and then blessed Abraham who, in return, offered him tithes of the spoils.

In accepting the blessing and in giving the tithe, Abraham recognized Melchizedek as priest and as his superior, and the author of Hebrews uses this to demonstrate the superiority of Melchizedek's priesthood over the Levitical priesthood which was superseded by it. The mystery of Melchizedek's origin is used as a prefiguration of the eternal priesthood of Christ. "The silence about the origin and destiny of Melchizedek, quite unusual in Scripture where we are so familiar with genealogical tables, makes him an appropriate figure of the Son of God, who as God had no mother and as Man no father, whose generation no man knows and whose eternal life is without beginning or end".[15]

In chapters 8-10 of the Epistle to the Hebrews, consideration is given to the way in which the Old Testament sacrifices and the Levitical priesthood were superseded by the perfect sacrifice and priesthood of Christ who is both Priest and Victim. By the obedience which he offered in the face of sin, Christians have been "sanctified through the offering of the body of Christ once for all"[16]. So the purposes of sacrifice and priesthood are fulfilled. In Christ men and women receive true forgiveness, the cost of which has been met by the blood of Christ, and are reconciled to God in him. "Having therefore, brethren, boldness to enter into the holy place by the blood of Jesus, by the way which he dedicated for us, a new and living way, through the veil, that is to say, his flesh; and having a great priest over the house of God, let us draw near with a true heart in fullness of faith".[17] The efficacy of the Cross and our 'acceptance in the beloved' make unnecessary the offering of sacrifice in order that we may merit the forgiveness of God and receive his grace: to suppose that we need to do so is to revert to the Old Testament and undermine the Gospel. For this reason, it is essential that the Church as a body and the members of it individually are, in worship and sacrament, enabled to live in continued recognition and acceptance of the fact that their relationship to God depends upon the eternal sacrifice of Christ, our great High Priest. The way in which that is made possible will be considered later in the context of the role of the ordained priesthood.

Meanwhile, three other passages of Scripture must be briefly considered, all of which link with the phrase in Hebrews "in the body of his flesh". The first is to be found in Chapter 2 of the First Epistle of Peter, and in particular verses 5 and 9. "Ye also, as living stones, are built up a spiritual house to be a holy priesthood, there offer up spiritual sacrifices acceptable to God through Jesus Christ" and "Ye are a chosen generation, a royal priesthood, an holy nation, a peculiar people; that ye should show forth the praises of him who called you out of darkness into his marvellous light"[18]. The second passage comes from the First Epistle of St Paul to the Corinthians, "The cup of blessing which we bless, is it not the communion of the blood of Christ? The bread which we break, is it not the communion of the body of Christ?"[19] The form of both questions indicates that an affirmative answer is expected. This passage must be considered in the context of what St Paul says after he has given his account of the Last Supper. "For as often as ye eat this bread and drink this cup, ye do show the Lord's death, till he come".[20] The third passage occurs in the same letter when St Paul, almost in passing, speaks of another way of understanding the significance of Our Lord's death, "Christ, our Passover is sacrificed for us; therefore let us keep the feast".[21]

The first passage makes it clear that the purpose of the Sacrifice and Resurrection of Christ which St Peter has considered in the preceding chapters is to bring into being a community which by virtue of what he has done is enabled to offer spiritual sacrifices to God. The fulfilment of what is thus made possible in Christ is expressed in the vision recorded in the Book of Revelation where creation is described as fulfilling itself by reflecting back to God in love his glory. "Every creature which is in heaven, and on earth, and under the earth and such as are in the sea, and all that are in them, heard I saying, 'Blessing and honour and power be unto him that sitteth upon the throne and unto the Lamb for ever and ever'".[22] The phrase "spiritual sacrifices" does not simply mean "Offerings of the mind or spirit" but applies to the whole person. St Paul appeals to us to offer our bodies as a living sacrifice, holy, acceptable to God, which is our reasonable service, or as the New English Bible translates it, the worship which we, as rational creatures, should offer. The sacrifices which Christians have to offer are made possible by the operation of the Holy Spirit who found in Christ the perfect instrument for his activity. The ability to offer such sacrifices depends upon our union with the risen Christ. This, as St Paul makes clear in the second passage, is possible because of the new Covenant established by the shedding of his blood, which is shown forth as often as we eat the bread and drink the cup of the Lord's Supper. United to Christ and made members of his Body by Baptism, we are sustained in our fellowship with him by the Communion of the body and blood of Christ.

The purpose of sacrifice is fulfilled in Christ. Communion with God is made possible for man, who is thus enabled to offer true sacrifice and be consecrated to God with creation of which he is part.

By his reference, in the third passage, to Christ as our Passover, St Paul brings out another aspect of sacrifice. In the Old Testament there are essentially two types of priesthood, the Levitical priesthood and, even then, the priesthood of the holy people of God. The Lamb for the Passover was slain by the Levitical priesthood, but the

Passover meal was celebrated by the father of the family, called to holiness. In the Last Supper the ritual act is one. Priest and Victim are one. Christ is the High Priest and he is the Victim. He slays the Passover Lamb, for his offering was a voluntary act, so that the family could share in the Passover and enter into the Promised Land. "God will himself provide the lamb".[23]

What then is the role of the ordained priesthood? Before answering that question two points need to be made, both of which relate to the fact that in Christ, human nature and the 'body of our flesh' is redeemed and consecrated to God. In that redemption and consecration the essential characteristics of human life are fulfilled and not denied. A human person lives because he has a body, created by God. With it and in it he lives in space and time and it is by his bodily actions that he expresses his spiritual nature. To live in the Spirit does not mean denying the body but allowing it to be used as an instrument of the Spirit. It is through his particular actions that a human person both expresses his intentions and gives them substance. To try to live a purely spiritual life in which ideas, hopes and aspirations alone are regarded as important is to deny the true nature of human existence. It is for this reason, therefore, not surprising that St Paul emphasizes that it was by the body of Christ that we are redeemed. It was in his body that his intentions of filial obedience were lived out.

In that body he rose again, in a way in which human nature is transfigured and as the resurrection appearances make clear, while continuous with our bodies in space and time, his body is released from the limitations which they lay upon it. So it was possible for him to share what he had done, and for human beings, living in space and time, to be united to him. The New Testament makes it clear that this sharing is effected by the power of God, not by the desires of men and

women. It is effected by the divine action in the
Eucharist. The Christian life is essentially a response to
the divine initiative in which what was achieved by God
in Christ is made available to us. It is because our
humanity is taken up into God and because we are still
men and women that the manner of our incorporation
into Christ and the manner by which we are nourished
in our life in Christ match the nature of our human
bodily existence.

Reading Church history it is all too evident that one
of the temptations which Christians have had to face is
the temptation to suppose that we have to establish
ourselves as worthy of merit in God's eyes, rather than
recognize that we are accepted as we are by the love of
God, and that it is by our response to his love that we
can walk worthy of our vocations.

In these days, that temptation takes the form of
seeking to make the operation of the divine love
dependent upon the ideas and attitudes of men, and to
suppose that pastoral care means giving people what
they want rather than declaring his will, which the
Gospel enables us to obey.

So it is that at the heart of the Church's life, and as its
most characteristic act, the Lord on the night before he
suffered, instituted the Eucharist, as means by which
our dependence on his saving acts is continually
affirmed. It was by that act that he gave the intention of
his forthcoming death. As Bishop A.E.J. Rawlinson
wrote in words which a Baptist theologian called, "one
of the truly seminal sentences in New Testament
Scholarship": "the doctrine of sacrifice (and of atonement) was not...read into the Last Supper; it was read
out of it. It was the Last Supper which afforded the
clue". It was there that "interpreting in advance the
significance of His coming Passion, He was in effect
making it to be for all time which it otherwise would
not have been, viz: a sacrifice for the sins of the world. It

is the Last Supper which makes Calvary sacrificial".[24] So the Church shows forth the Lord's death till he come again.

The Eucharist is not the creation of the Church, a rite which it devised as liturgy to be helpful. It was instituted by Our Lord and given to the Church, so that men and women might for ever be able to respond to the Divine initiative. As Cyril, Bishop of Jerusalem in the second half of the fourth century, said, when addressing those who were to be baptized, "Baptism is the ending of the old covenant and the beginning of the new",[25] and "For just 'as the children are partakers of the flesh and blood, he also himself likewise took part'[26] with them, so that we, by partaking in his presence after the flesh, may also become partakers of his divine grace."[27]

The Church on earth can only live in a way which is true to its nature if it is dependent upon Christ as the eternal High Priest and Shepherd of the flock. It is, by its very nature, essentially sacramental. In the context of the New Covenant that word means much more than the fact that the created universe, being created by God, reflects his nature. In the church of the new Covenant on earth, the Lord uses the substances of creation, re-created in him and made the instrument of his will, as the means by which his new life is communicated to men and women, and in such a way that they are enabled to come to God relying on the promises and power of God and without presuming on their own righteousness. So the two Sacraments ordained by the Lord himself are constitutive of the Church and enable it to grow into Christ. As well as these two Sacraments, the Lord called the Apostles to a unique role in the Church by which it was to be recalled constantly to its dependence upon Christ and to the fact that it was the Lord's Church belonging to him. It does not belong to its members with the corollary that they can adopt it to suit their desires.

Space does not permit consideration of the way in which the development took place in the first centuries by which the unique ministry of the Apostles became a priestly ministry within the Church. It must suffice to say that the "institution was shaped by the Gospel itself-that is, by the once-for-all fact of Christ in history and the knowledge of Christ's continuing ministry which together form the substance of the Christian message. It was the pressure of Gospel truth concerning Christ and his work that caused the church to feel the need for episcopal office once the uniquely comprehensive and authoritative oversight of the Apostles had ceased, and caused the development of the office to be accepted without demure (so far as we know) everywhere".[28]

The essential role of the priesthood was beautifully expressed in 1652 by George Herbert in his classic work 'A Priest to the Temple': "A priest is the deputy of Christ for the reducing of man to the obedience of God". More than 300 years later in 1973 the Group Des Dombes, comprising Roman Catholic, Lutheran and Reformed theologians in France and Switzerland, defined the pastoral office as securing and symbolically representing the dependence of the Church on Christ.

The author of the Epistle to the Hebrews speaks of Our Lord as "the Apostle and High Priest of our profession".[29] By this Apostleship, the Apostles were charged with the duty of witnessing to the Apostleship and High Priesthood of Christ. So St Paul calls himself a "priest" (leitourgos) of Christ Jesus, performing the priestly role of ministering the Gospel of God, so that the Gentiles might become an acceptable offering (prosphora) to God. So, also, in the early ordination rites, the role of a bishop is associated with the High Priesthood of Christ, through whom the Church is enabled to be offered in him. (The same applies to the priests or presbyters with whom bishops share their episcopate, delegating some powers to them.)

It is sometimes said that "having fulfilled the ancient covenant, Christ brought about a change from the cultic to the personal. Cultic sacrifice no longer had any worth except through Jesus' personal sacrifice".[30] It is difficult to justify these sentences in the light of the Biblical doctrine of man, implying as they do that the cultic was abolished by Christ. In fact, the institution of Baptism and the Eucharist represent the transformation, not the abolition, of the cultic.

The cultic represents a fundamental Biblical principle, fulfilled supremely in the Incarnation. It is the principle that God deals with men through chosen individuals; particular acts in particular places for the benefit of all men everywhere. The abandonment of that principle leads into a kind of gnosticism, by which attitudes of mind become paramount and the wholeness of human nature as embodied spirit is denied. It would be much more accurate and in accordance with Biblical thought to say that Christ gave new content to the cultic. By his personal sacrifice, cultic sacrifice was given new worth and the personal offering it represented was made possible.

By his calling of the Apostles and by his institution of the Eucharist, Our Lord gave to his Church a structure by which it could be enabled to be sustained in its union with him, and witness to his unique High Priesthood. By his ordination, a man is set in a new relationship to Christ in his Body the Church, with the particular role of being the sacramental sign of the fact that Christ is Head of the Church and depends for its being and life upon the sacrifice of Christ. As celebrant of the Eucharist, he is the instrument through whom the death and resurrection of Christ is shown forth. When he absolves the sinner, he witnesses to the fact that it is Christ who forgives.

The advocates of the ordination of women to the

priesthood sometimes argue that since Our Lord, though male, redeemed both men and women, this fact should be represented by having both a male and a female priesthood. Such a notion raises most disturbing questions about the Incarnation itself. If, in order to be truly representative of Our Lord, both a male and a female priesthood is necessary, how can Christ himself be said to have shared our humanity completely. The logic of the advocates' argument would seem to require not just a male and a female priesthood but a second Incarnation in which God took the nature and body of a female to live on earth. It follows that, meanwhile, our redemption is incomplete and that the Gospel which the Church has been proclaiming for nearly two thousand years is inadequate. It also seems to require the conclusion that neither a man nor a woman alone can be said to be fully human or representative of another.

It is sometimes said that a priest is the representative of the people, but such an understanding of Christian priesthood is not to be found in the early ordination rites, in the Ordinal of the Book of Common Prayer, or in that of the Alternative Service Book of the Church of England. To suppose that he is represents a reversion to the idea of sacrifice in the Old Testament in which the priest does symbolically on behalf of the people what they cannot do for themselves. His role is to be the instrument through whom grace is given so that they may truly be offered in Christ.

As Karl Rahner has pointed out, the priestly ministry is essentially ministry to the Church. "The priesthood of the official priest is accordingly purely a ministerial one both in relation to the active existential priesthood of Christ and to the passive existential priesthood of the faithful, in so far as it makes a permanent sacramental presence possible to both."[31]

The Christian priest indeed "taken from among men, is appointed for men in things pertaining to God". But he is so appointed to relate the perfect sacrifice of Christ to the community which has "its origin and continued life in that Sacrifice". Through the action of the priest as celebrant, the community is enabled to "show forth the Lord's death till he come, to proclaim its dependence upon its Lord and, receiving the fruits of his Passion, therein set forth, to be offered in mind, body and spirit, a living sacrifice, acceptable to God". As Father Jean Tillard has said, "Thanks to this priesthood the community can sit at the table where the sacrificial death of the unique priest is celebrated"[32] and so is enabled to fulfil its mission to the world and give glory to God.

Notes

1. *Theological Investigations - Vol IV E.T.*, Darton, Longman and Todd. 1967, p.242
2. *The Mind and Heart of Love*, 2nd Edition, Fontana p.322
3. 1 John 4,10
4. *"Suffering"*. Darton, Longman and Todd 1973, p.36
5. Apostolic Office: Sacrament of Christ. Edward J. Kilmartin, S.J. Theological Studies Vol 36 No. 2 (1975) p.255
6. *The Foundations of New Testament Christology*. Fontana 1969 p.248
7. *Ephesians II.8*
8. *Article XXV*
9. *Hebrews 1.1*
10. *Hebrews 1,2-3*
11. *op.cit. 3,1-6*
12. *op.cit. 12,14*
13. *op.cit. 5,4*
14. *op.cit. 5.8*
15. *Christ, Priesthood and the Liturgy*. R.J. Foster Goodliffe Neal 1973 p.30
16. *Hebrews 10.10*
17. *Hebrews 10,19-22*
18. *1 Peter 2, 5 and 9*
19. *1 Corinthians 10,16*
20. *1 Corinthians, 12.26*
21. *1 Corinthians 5, 7-8*
22. *Revelation 5.13*
23. *Genesis 22.8*
24. *Mysterium Christi*, ed. G.K.A. Bell and A. Deissman 1930, p.241
25. *Catechetical Lecture III.6*
26. *Hebrews 2.14*

27. *Catechetical Lecture III.11*
28. *Growing into Union, Buchanan, Leonard, Mascall and Packer SPCK 1970 p.75*
29. *Hebrews 3.1*
30. *e.g. Leon Dufour Dictionary of the New Testament s.v. priest*
31. *op.cit. p.250*
32. *What Priesthood has the Ministry? Grove Books 1973 p.27*

Women and Ordination

Joyce A. Little, Ph.D.

When Betty Friedan, author of *The Feminine Mystique*, was asked some years ago what she thought the most important effect of feminism would be, she responded, "I can't tell you now. You wouldn't believe it anyhow . . . it is theological."[1]

When feminists turned their attention to the Catholic Church, the most obvious evidence of sexual inequality seemed clearly to be the Church's refusal to admit women to the ordained priesthood and, by extension, to the institutional hierarchy of the Church. Not only a significant number of nuns, but also a good many priests and male theologians, agreed with them. For a great many Catholics, the arguments for women's ordination seemed, virtually overnight, to become obvious and inescapable. In this essay, I will first, examine what seem to me to be the three major arguments in support of women's ordination and the reasons why these arguments fail to reflect not only Catholic teachings on the priesthood but also the Catholic understanding of human sexuality; second, the radically opposed visions of reality which underlie Catholicism, on the one hand, and feminism, on the other; and finally, a brief preliminary indication of the nature and importance of the role of women in the Church.

The first major argument feminists raise in defense of women's ordination is based primarily on feminist experience itself. Feminists argue that the lack of female priests on the altar and female bishops in the hierarchy gives women a sense of inferiority, of second class citizenship within the Church and further, that many Catholic women experience a call to ordination which is frustrated by the Church's refusal to recognize it. They argue, in effect, that the Church, by refusing to ordain women, finds herself in opposition to the Holy Spirit, who is calling women to the priesthood.

Several assumptions underlie this argument, two of which deserve our special attention. The first of these is the notion that the Holy Spirit calls whom He (or, as many feminists would say, "She") will, and the Church has no right to impede the movements of the Spirit. This view that the Spirit operates not within the Church, but in opposition to her, is entirely at loggerheads with the Catholic faith which holds that the Holy Spirit is the gift of Christ to the Catholic Church, which Christ established and within which he remains really, sacramentally present in the Eucharist. Just as God became visibly present and united to us in the visible, material humanity of Christ, so he remains visibly present and united to us in the visible, material structures and sacraments of the Church. To separate the activities of the Holy Spirit from any visible, material anchor in history is to deny the enduring character of the Incarnation in history. Furthermore, to place the Church in opposition to the workings of the Holy Spirit raises doubts as to whether Christ can be actually present within such a Church, doubts which many feminist theologians have not hesitated to entertain. The issue of women's ordination, at this point, involves its supporters in suppositions about how God must be seen to act which undermine the central teachings of the Catholic faith with regard to Christ, the

Holy Spirit and the Church.

The second assumption which underlies the feminist argument from experience is the view that the contemporary experience of feminist women is more fundamental to understanding reality than is the worship and tradition of the Church. If feminists recognize anything to be infallible, it is their own experience, not the experience of the Church. If they recognize anything to be revelatory, it is feminism itself, not the revelation given in Christ. As Rosemary Radford Ruether, a prominent feminist theologian who continues to call herself a Catholic, has said,

> The uniqueness of feminist theology lies not in its use of the criterion of experience but rather in its use of *women's* experience, which has been almost entirely shut out of theological reflection in the past. The use of women's experience in feminist theology, therefore, explodes as a critical force, exposing classical theology, including its codified traditions, as based on *male* experience rather than on universal human experience.[2]

The "classical theology" and "codified traditions" which Ruether supposes to be exposed by feminist theology include such things as papal and conciliar teachings, the universal and traditional practices of the Church and, indeed, the Bible itself.[3]

At this point, it is not only useful but essential to recall a few things the Church has to say about vocations to the ordained priesthood. First, no one has a right to be a priest. The initiative does not lie with us, but with Christ, who calls whom he will to ordination. Second, the Church never simply accepts at face value the claims anyone might make to having experienced such a call. Human experience is not infallible, and many a man in the two thousand year history of the Church has misinterpreted God's will for him with regard to ordination. We are therefore not obliged to accept as infallible the claims anyone, man or woman, makes to be called to ordination. Third, the Church understands her own tradition (which is to say her own experience) to be a more fundamental criterion than the experience of any group within or without the Church when it comes to discerning the will of God and the movements of the Holy Spirit. Those who claim that the Church refuses to ordain women because Christ himself refused to do so are certainly not entirely wrong, but they are also not entirely right. For the Church appeals not only to the actions of Christ, but also to her own actions, her own experience, her own tradition, as guided by the Eucharistic Christ and the indwelling Spirit.

The importance which Catholicism gives to tradition has enormous bearing on the second major argument feminists give for women's ordination, since the second argument, unlike the first, is based on Scripture. The argument at first glance seems unexceptional and irrefutable. Citing Genesis, feminists point out that all of us, male and female, are made in the image of God. We are equal before God. Christianity, they then go on to point out, not only accepts this but reiterates it in a striking fashion in Galatians 3:28, where St Paul tells us that "There is neither Jew nor Greek, there is neither slave nor free, there is neither male nor female; for you are all one in Christ Jesus." From this Scripturally-based insistence upon the equality of all human beings, feminists conclude to a non-differentiation between male and female. Hence, they maintain that, since the fact that Christ chose only Jewish apostles did not stop the Church from ordaining Gentile priests, then the fact that Christ chose only male apostles should not stop the Church from ordaining female priests.

The difficulty with this argument does not lie, of course, in the view that men and women are equal. With this the Church agrees. The difficulty lies in associating sexual equality with sexual identity. With this the Church does not agree. Male and female not only can but should be differentiated from one another. The question at issue here is a matter not only of faith but of common sense as well. Equality and identity do not, in fact, go hand in hand. A moment's reflection will confirm this. Words like "inferior" and "superior" can only be applied to things which are in some fashion identical. One football player, for example, can be called superior to another football player, because they are both football players. One mystery writer can be recognized as better than another mystery writer, because both are mystery writers. But we do not ordinarily say that this football player is better than that mystery writer. To do so would be, as the popular expression puts it, like comparing apples and oranges. We can only compare and recognize inequalities in those things which are fundamentally identical. Sexual identity will not promote male/female equality, it will only promote male/female competition.

On theological grounds, such a notion of identity is incompatible with both Scripture and tradition, and we need look only at Scripture to see this. On the surface, the text from Galatians may seem to suggest that the difference between male and female has, like the distinctions between Jew and Gentile and slave and free, been removed by Christ. However, when we examine the rest of Scripture, we discover an important difference governing the relationship between male and female, on the one hand, and Jew and Gentile or slave and free, on the other. In Genesis, we are told that God created the human race male and female. He did not, however, create us Jew and Gentile, slave and free. These are differences which, in the Old Testament, arise after and as a consequence of original sin. As one theologian notes,

. . . while being male and female is an ontological

reality in the order of creation, nationality and slavery are not. They are rather human conditions which are the result of sin. They have no ontological, theological, sacramental or eschatological substance. They have no place in the sacramental structure and life of the Church. God did not create humans to be Jews or Greeks, neither did he make them to be slaves or freemen. He did make them male and female, however, and although the spiritual and moral divisions between the sexes are overcome in Christ, the ontological differences are not.[4]

Furthermore, when we examine the Galatians text within the larger context of what St Paul is explicitly addressing, we discover that the point he is making has reference to baptism, not to ordination. For, in the immediately preceding verse (v. 27), St Paul says, "For as many of you as were baptized into Christ have put on Christ." Although the text does not specifically mention priesthood at all, we are well within our rights to see it as relevant to the royal priesthood of all believing Christians, the priesthood to which we gain access by baptism and which we share alike, male and female, Jew and Gentile, slave and free. But we have no warrant at all for applying this text to the ordained priesthood.

Scripture also has something very important to tell us about the verdict of tradition on this matter. The New Testament is, we must remember, not only a record of the revelation given by Christ in his historic ministry; it is also a record of the revelation as given in the work of the apostles and in the life of the Apostolic Church following the ascension of Christ into heaven. For the revelation does not close with Christ's death, resurrection and ascension, but rather extends to the close of the Apostolic age. What the Church did in that first generation of Christian faith and worship has entered into the Word of God and become normative for all subsequent generations. As a theologian of the Greek Orthodox Church has pointed out,

> The Gospel of Christ cannot be written anew because "the fullness of time" came then and not at any other time. There is a sense in which all Christians must become Christ's contemporaries. Therefore, the very "historical conditioning" which characterizes the Gospel of Christ is, in a sense, *normative for us*. The twentieth century is not an absolute norm; the apostolic age is.[5]

The point made by that theologian is important for our purposes here today, because while it is true, as feminists say, that Christ appointed only Jewish and only male apostles, when we examine the activities of the early Church as recorded in the New Testament, we discover that the Church herself decided, in that first generation, that Christians are not bound to circumcision and other requirements of the Jewish law. This decision, recorded in the 15th chapter of the Acts of the Apostles, was made by the Apostles gathered together in Jerusalem and acting under the guidance of the Holy Spirit. Their meeting, dubbed by Scripture scholars as the "Apostolic Council", opened the doors to ordaining Gentiles. The Apostolic Church, however, made no corresponding decision with regard to women. Hence, neither Scripture itself nor the earliest traditions of the Church, as recorded in Scripture, provide any warrant for women's ordination. Add to this the following nineteen centuries of Church tradition denying women access to ordination, and we are confronted with an extraordinarily long and consistent testimony against such a practice.

Feminists maintain at this point that what we really have here is a male-dominated hierarchy trying desperately to maintain its patriarchal authority. But the basic issue at hand runs much deeper than that. For what is called into question when we doubt the validity of

Church tradition is not just an arbitrary male authority run amuck for some 2000 years. What is called into question is the nature of the Church and indeed the trustworthiness of revelation itself. For how are we to trust the Church as "the pillar and ground of the truth", as I Timothy calls her, if she is capable of committing and adhering to such an error for 20 centuries? How are we to trust that the Holy Spirit will lead us into all truth, as John's Gospel tells us, if we have been so badly led for so long that we now require the guidance of the feminist movement to lead us to the truth? How are we to take seriously Christ's words in Matthew that He shall be with us always, if evidence for his presence is so lacking in the life and worship of the Church? Indeed, in the final analysis, how are we to take seriously the Bible in which these words are recorded, when the words seem to have so little bearing on reality? It should come as no surprise that leading feminist theologians who continue to call themselves Catholic, such as Rosemary Radford Ruether and Elizabeth Schussler Fiorenza, no longer take any of these things seriously. What we face here is not a crisis of authority. It is a crisis of faith.

In the final analysis, the feminist notion that women ought to be ordained because they, as much as men, image God, fails precisely because it does not address the key issue of Church teaching regarding the ordained priesthood. The key issue relates to Christ, not to God. The priest acts in the person of Christ (*in persona Christi*), not in the person of God. Hence, the question at issue is not whether women and men equally image God, but whether women and men equally image Christ. And to that question, the Church has consistently answered no. Because Christ stands to the Church as bridegroom to bride, and because the priest acts in the person of Christ, whose role is specifically male vis-a-vis the Church, women are not able to stand in Christ's place or to act in His person. Indeed, the marriage of Christ with his Church lies at the foundation not only of the Church's teachings on the ordained priesthood, but also of her insistence upon the differentiated and complementary character of male and female sexuality, a fact which brings us to the third major feminist argument regarding women's ordination.

The third argument consists of an open criticism of and even attack upon Scripture, tradition and Church teachings. The focus of the attack is the now often-quoted text from chapter 5 of Paul's letter to the Ephesians, where we are given the following instruction:

Be subject to one another, out of reverence for Christ. Wives, be subject to your husbands, as to the Lord. For the husband is the head of the wife as Christ is the head of the church, his body, and is himself its Saviour. As the church is subject to Christ, so let wives also be subject in everything to their husbands. Husbands, love your wives, as Christ loved the church and gave himself up for her, that he might sanctify her, having cleansed her by the washing of water with the word, that he might present the church to himself in splendour, without spot or wrinkle or any such thing, that she might be holy and without blemish. Even so husbands should love their wives as their own bodies. He who loves his wife loves himself. For no man ever hates his own flesh, but nourishes and cherishes it, as Christ does the church, because we are members of his body. "For this reason a man shall leave his father and mother and be joined to his wife, and the two shall become one flesh." This mystery is a profound one, and I am saying that it refers to Christ and the church; however, let each one of you love his wife as himself, and let the wife see that she respects her husband. (Eph 5:21-33)

Both Ruether and Fiorenza see the Bible in general to be distorted by male chauvinism, and this passage in particular to offer clear evidence of patriarchal domination over women. Ruether comments on it as follows:

In the New Testament, the [Old Testament] hierarchical pattern of divine male over human female as an analogy for patriarchal marriage is not only continued but exaggerated. This is particularly evident in the post-Pauline letter to the Ephesians (chapter 5). Here the headship of Christ over the Church is the model for the proper relationship of paternalistic husband and submissive wife in Christian marriage. By making the husband analogous to Christ in relation to his wife, the author even suggests that a wife should consider her husband representative of Christ or God! Her husband is her Lord, as Christ is Lord of the Church. She is his body, as the Church is the body of Christ.[6]

Fiorenza is no kinder.

The relationship between Christ and the church, expressed in the metaphors of head and body as well as of bridegroom and bride, becomes the paradigm for Christian marriage and vice versa. This theological paradigm reinforces the cultural-patriarchal pattern or subordination, insofar as the relationship between Christ and church clearly is not a relationship between equals, since the church-bride is totally dependent and subject to her head or bridegroom. Therefore, the general injunction for all members of the Christian community, "Be subject to one another in the fear of Christ," is clearly spelled out for the Christian wife as requiring submission and inequality.[7]

Both of these theologians see this passage as paradigmatic for understanding how tradition has operated within Catholicism. According to them, a patriarchal reading of marriage as the domination of male over female was deliberately introduced into Scripture by men and used by them ever since to justify their own chauvinistic assumptions about male superiority, skewing in the process a proper understanding of both the Christ-Church and the male-female relationships, not to mention marriage and the priesthood as well. History, as the feminists never tire of telling us, is the record of the victors, and where the history of the Church is concerned, men have, according to them, enjoyed a long and virtually unbroken string of triumphs.[8] It is difficult to imagine a more encompassing or more destructive critique of Catholicism than we have here.

Before considering how we might better understand the passage from Ephesians, especially in terms of the role women are called to play in the Church, I would like to pause here a moment to consider the quite different views of reality which distinguish feminism from Catholicism. Women on both sides of the ordination debate openly acknowledge the incompatibility of feminism and traditional Christian faith. Rosemary Radford Ruether noted, in the July 5, 1985, issue of the *National Catholic Reporter*, with reference to the two year dialogue between the Women's Ordination Conference and the Catholic Bishops' Committee on Women, that "What soon became obvious to us [the Women's Ordination Conference] was the vast gap between our consciousness and theirs [the bishops] not only on matters such as theology and morality, but even on matters of fact. We simply had an entirely different picture of the reality of the Church and its history."[9]

Ruether goes on to say that the women in the Women's Ordination Conference took the view that Jesus was a Messiah figure within Judaism, that the movement carried on by his disciples after his death (no mention is made of his resurrection and ascension, and indeed Ruether has elsewhere denied that we have any

firm reason for believing in personal life after death[10])
was not initially an institution or Church at all, and
therefore any attempt to say that Jesus founded the
institutional Church with its hierarchical structures is
"like saying that Sitting Bull founded the Bureau of
Indian Affairs."[11] She concludes that feminists and
bishops are "not only talking differently about the same
things, but in some very basic ways we are really talking
about different things when we use words such as
'Christ' and the 'church'."[12]

Deborah Belonick, a Greek Orthodox theologian
opposed to feminist theology, sees the same radical
dichotomy between feminism and that Christian faith
which is rooted in the Bible and the councils of the
Church. According to her,

> This feminist theology is in fact so opposed to the
> Bible and tradition of the Christian Church that
> one may say that two different worldviews, two
> visions of God and humanity, are present. And
> since there is such a wide divergence between the
> two theological systems, only *one* can claim to be
> truly in the Spirit of Jesus Christ; the two view-
> points are too distinct for both to be called
> "Christian." One is forced to speak either in the
> category of "feminist-liberationist priesthood" or
> of "male-Christian priesthood," when given the
> fact that the female priesthood is based on a
> theology in opposition to traditional doctrines of
> the Church and the creative and salvific acts of
> God.[13]

Feminism proceeds on the assumption that anything
which contradicts modern female experience as interpreted by feminists must be wrong. This means that the
revelation of Christ as mediated to us by the Church
through her tradition, through conciliar and papal
teachings, through the Bible, must submit itself to
feminist scrutiny; that the feminists may separate the

wheat from the chaff, the sheep from the goats. To accept such a view is, of course, to accept the dismantling of the Catholic Church.

Being Catholic does not mean we have to deny the presence of male chauvinism in the Church, either in the past or in the present. Catholicism teaches that all of us are fallen, men and women alike, and male chauvinism is a consequence of male fallenness. The Catholic Church, however, also teaches that, in Christ, the fullness of the divine revelation is given. That revelation is manifested to us, first, through the visible, material humanity of Christ, and, second, through the visible, material structures and sacraments of the Church. The Eucharistic Christ and the Indwelling Spirit guarantee that human sinfulness, male and female alike, shall not undermine the way, the truth and the life, who is Christ, and the Church, which is his Spouse. This is our faith as Catholics. If we do not believe this, we cannot properly speak of ourselves as Catholic.

Although feminists began by calling into question the Church's male priesthood, they have ended by calling into question the Church herself, and, by extension, the whole of the Christian revelation as mediated to us through the Church. Women's ordination has become the tip of an iceberg which would sink the Church more rapidly than that which sunk the Titanic. To quote Deborah Belonick once again, ". . . admitting women to the priesthood should not be the main issue of debate . . . . The question is much deeper than that. The point is that the theological arguments supporting the ordination of women ultimately are opposed to the Christian faith and its teachings about salvation."[14]

If it be correct to say that the theological arguments supporting women's ordination wreak havoc with our faith, and I believe that they do, then what do theological arguments opposing women's ordination have to offer us by way of a positive understanding of

the role of women in the Church which is consistent
with our faith? If the role of women cannot be directly
identified with the priestly activity of Christ as carried
on by those who are explicitly ordained to do so, then
how are we to understand our role? Any attempt to
answer this question is fraught with difficulties, if only
because so little has been done in this area. We must
keep in mind that, until recently, theology was done
almost exclusively by men, and ordained men at that,
many of whom were blatantly chauvinistic and most of
whom had little or no interest in this matter. Even
today, very few theologians are much interested in
pursuing an explicitly theological and even Christocentric account of the covenantal relationship of men and
women.[15] Yet it is precisely this covenantal relationship
which must be understood if we are to counter the
feminist view of women with an explicitly Catholic
one.

In the Ephesians text quoted earlier, we have one of
the most profound statements in the New Testament
regarding the male/female relationship. St Paul tells us
there that human marriage images the Christ/Church
relationship. This is an enormously important point,
because most of us, I suspect, tend to think just the
opposite. We tend to suppose that human marriage is
the primary reality, and that St Paul borrows imagery
from it to describe in a metaphorical fashion the close
relationship between Christ and His Church. Such,
however, is not the case. St Paul intends us to
understand that the fundamental marriage, upon which
all human marriages are based, is the marriage between
Christ and the Church. That is the great "mystery", as
he calls it. The fundamental, underlying structure of our
existence as human beings is marital. Human marriages
are themselves an image of this deeper, most profound
reality of our very being. What St Paul has to say about
human marriages, therefore, cannot be dismissed as a

piece of male chauvinism. It must be taken with utmost seriousness, even if we find ourselves made very uncomfortable by the language he employs. And I don't think one need be a feminist to find the language somewhat offputting.

The difficulties for women come in the first few lines of the passage. Although it seems to get off to a good start, stating that husbands and wives are to be subject to one another, it goes on to say that wives ought to be subject to their husbands, indeed ought to be subject "in everything" to their husbands, because the husband is the head of the wife just as Christ is head of the Church. The fact that husbands are later on enjoined to love their wives, as Christ loves the Church, does little to mitigate the feeling that women are placed in a position which is, as the feminists are the first to point out, submissive and dependent.

Before we rush to assume that what Paul has in mind here is sexual inequality, with women getting the short end of the stick, we ought to consider two things very carefully. First, we cannot assume, as feminists do, that Paul's language here can be taken at face value, that is, can be understood as we popularly understand such language. As Donald J. Keefe, a Jesuit theologian at Marquette, has noted,

> Paul's language can be understood only when one keeps firmly in mind that its meaning is governed not by ordinary usage or by ordinary common sense; these are not in service of the revelation which he serves. Paul's use of such antagonistic words as fear, submission and the like, to describe the appropriate reaction of the Christian wife to her husband is entirely misunderstood when it is forgotten that we do not know what this language means in any adequate sense.[16]

The second point, closely related to the first, is that we do have some indication, from the teachings of the

Church herself, that notions such as dependence and submission do not automatically signal inequality. For these words apply to Christ's relationship with the Father. We see this very clearly in the Gospel of John alone, where we are told that the Son is dependent on the Father ("the Son can do nothing of His own accord, but only what he sees the Father doing" – 5:19), receptive vis-a-vis the Father ("All that the Father has is mine" – 16:15), submissive to the Father, that is, under a mission given him by the Father ("I came not of my own accord, but He sent me" – 8:42) and obedient to the Father ("I do as the Father has commanded me" – 14:31). If dependence and submission, not to mention receptivity and obedience, signal inferiority, then Christ must be inferior to the Father, as indeed many theologians in the early Church maintained. Their view, known as Arianism, was explicitly and flatly rejected by the Church in the fourth century councils of Nicaea and Constantinople, in which the Son was recognized to be consubstantial with and equal in all ways to the Father.

The language which St Paul uses to describe the male/female relationship is therefore consistent with the language which Christ employs in the Gospel of John to describe His own relationship with the Father. The language does not signify inferiority; it signifies relationality, which is to say order, and that order which such language signifies reveals to us that, at the highest and most profound level, that is, in the Trinity itself, order is the very complement of equality. The two go hand in hand.

The Ephesians text, therefore, does not support arguments for male superiority. On the contrary, it reveals to us, first, that the covenantal, which is to say, the marital relationship of Christ and the Church is the fundamental structure of all human relationships, and, second, that the covenantal structure is the basis for our imaging of the order and relationality which is found in the Trinity. The role of women in the Church cannot, therefore, be divorced (if you will pardon the pun) either from marriage itself or from that activity which is proper to the Church as the bride of Christ.

Beyond this point, we find ourselves at the frontier of territory which has, unfortunately been little explored by theologians to date. Hence, anything further which might be said with regard to the bridal character of the Church and to the implications this has for women in the Church must necessarily be more by way of suggestion than by way of already-established theological conclusions.

Three matters ought immediately to command our consideration. The first of these is the fact that, although masculinity is given an exclusive expression in the sacrament of holy orders, femininity is given no such corresponding exclusive expression. This sacramental practice of the Church finds an important confirmation in the historic ministry of Christ, in the fact that, although the Blessed Virgin Mary, who is identified with the Church, enjoyed a relationship to her Son closer than any of the Apostles, she was not called upon by her Son to share in their explicit apostolic ministry. Since this state of affairs does not signal her inferiority to the Apostles, might it not signify instead that femininity, and by extension, the uniqueness of female roles in the Church, require no special, exclusive, sacramental expression?

This brings us to the second matter we ought to consider, namely, the importance of the Blessed Virgin Mary in the life and teachings of the Church. Karl Stern, a psychologist and convert to Catholicism, has noted that, whereas the dominant note in the Old Testament is that of prophecy, which is to say, an emphasis on God's future activity in history, the dominant note of the New Testament is Incarnation, which is to say, God's here-and-now or realized presence within history and humanity. As Stern puts it,

> In the Hebrew Liturgy, the patriarchs are invoked, as the Blessed Virgin is in the Christian. The remote foreknowledge of that which one will neither see nor touch, is the paternal. Nevertheless, as we have seen, Israel, and mankind as a whole, men and women, represent the Bride. And it is with the Incarnation as historical fact that the Blessed Virgin becomes the prototype of faith. Here, contrary to the faith of the prophets, faith achieves the immediacy of certitude, in that carnal link with being which is the core of all womanhood.[17]

Stern here makes two points which are crucial. First, the Incarnational character of Christianity is linked to the female because she, more than the male, is herself linked with the material and the biological. And the material and the biological lie at the very heart of the sacramental notion that materiality can and does mediate the divine.

The second, and equally important, point is that all of us, male and female alike, are represented by the feminine principle, first, by Mary's *fiat* which is spoken on behalf of us all, and, second, by the Church, which as Bride of Christ incorporates both men and women into that marital union which the Church enjoys with Christ. The implications are obviously sacramental. Just as Mary, by her consent, makes it possible for God to be ontologically united with and materially present among us, so the Church, by her consent, makes it possible for Christ to be ontologically united with and visibly, materially, and institutionally present within the history of the world. For this reason, Hans Urs von Balthasar could say that "the feminine, Marian principle is, in the Church, what encompasses all other principles, even the Petrine."[14]

The third matter which ought to command our

attention is the nature of the differentiation between male and female. Walter Ong, a Jesuit in St Louis, has pointed out that masculinity is hard to interiorize, because the masculine is so much identified with the objective and the transcendent.[19] If this be the case, and I believe that it is, the difficulty which faces femininity, which is identified with the subjective and immanent, is that of finding ways to objectify or externalize it. Because the female finds her femininity within herself and indeed because she herself is most closely linked with all that is immanent in creation, femininity by its nature tends to resist all attempts to assign to it a specific objective role. This is particularly true with regard to the sacramentality of the Church, where the feminine, as the matrix of all of the sacraments, is difficult, if not impossible, to externalize in any single role which would seek to embody once and for all the relationship of the feminine to the sacraments.

Some efforts have been made, mostly by men (perhaps not surprisingly, if we have been correct in identifying the male with the objective), to objectify the differences between male and female. Kierkegaard, for example, said "Woman is substance, man is reflexion."[20] Louis Bouyer, the French Catholic theologian, in his book on women in the church, speaks variously of men as identified with apostolate and women with presence,[21] of men associated with formal prescription and of women with influence,[22] and of men as representing the gift of God in the transcendence of the giver while women represent the receptivity of the gift in the deepest levels of human being.[23] Presence, receptivity, and influence all suggest that which cannot be sacramentally objectified.

However the role of women is to be understood in the Church, it must always be by reference to the marital imagery which understands human relationships to be modeled on those of the Christ-Church relationship. As C.S. Lewis pointed out several years ago, in the introduction to Louis Bouyer's book on women in the church (to which reference was earlier made),

> One of the ends for which sex was created was to symbolize to us the hidden things of God. One of the functions of human marriage is to express the nature of the union between Christ and the Church. We have no authority to take the living and semitive figures which God has painted on the canvas of our nature and shift them about as if they were mere geometrical figures.
> This is what common sense will call "mystical." Exactly. The Church claims to be the bearer of a revelation. If that claim is false then we want not to make priestesses but to abolish priests.[24]

The marital imagery employed by St Paul is a "mystery," as St Paul himself tells us. Karl Stern refers to it as "The unspeakable mystery of the *and* - of God *and* His Creation, of God *and* His people, of Christ *and* the Church."[25] Man *and* woman share in that mysterious "and", of course, but the mystery runs far deeper than that. For, as Stern rightly points out, "The sexual 'and' is a reflection of the other - all being is nuptial."[26]

These brief reflections fall far short of any sort of definitive presentation of the role of women in the Church. Much more work must be done in this area, and must be done quickly, if feminism is to be answered. For, in the final analysis, feminism challenges the Church on every level of her being. As Ruether herself has noted, "it is not possible to imagine the admission of women to the Catholic priesthood without, at the same time, modifying certain fundamental notions about hierarchy, theology, Church and authority."[27] Ruether's use of the word "modifying" is an enormous understatement. The changes, as noted earlier, would dismantle the Church.

Sometimes the feminine is associated with total,

unconditional love. Walter Ong expresses beautifully how such total love is conveyed by the Pieta, and I would like to close this paper with his description of that statue.

> In the Pieta the Virgin Mother has freed herself of all possessiveness, transmuted all eros (love involved in its own need) into agape (love as self-giving, involved with the other). She has done so by lovingly acquiescing to her now adult Son's doing what he was called to do, his Father's will. She leaves her Son completely free, though doing so returns him dead to her arms. And when she takes him dead into her arms, she does not clutch him, but leaves her arms open. The statue tugs at the hearts of women and men alike, but its subject matter is supremely feminine. And it is supreme human freedom: Mary has deliberately chosen to let her Son be about his Father's business. If she had the choice once more, knowing what it would cost, she would do it again. No regrets. Total courage. Her youthful choice is still part of her. Hence her youthful face, often commented on, despite her mature age. Her arms are open and relaxed. She is completely free, for she is fully aware of what she has chosen.[28]

Catholic women today are confronted with a choice - the choice between feminism, on the one hand, and Catholicism, on the other. We, the women of the Church, which is the Bride of Christ, are called upon today, in a way in which we have never been called upon before, to speak in the person of the Church (*in persona Ecclesiae*). If we choose, as I have argued here that we ought, to let Christ be about his Father's business today through the traditional and institutional life and worship of the Catholic Church, we too should do so freely, fully aware of what we are choosing and why.[29]

Notes

1. Betty Friedan, *The Feminine Mystique*, quoted in "The Spirit of the Female Priesthood", by Deborah Belonick, in Thomas Hopko (ed.), *Women and the Priesthood* (Crestwood, NY: St Vladimir's Seminary Press, 1983), p. 135.
2. Rosemary Radford Ruether, *Sexism and God-Talk* (Boston: Beacon Press, 1983), p. 13.
3. Ruether makes her objections to the institution and tradition of Catholicism more than clear when discussing how feminist methodology goes about overcoming the corruption which it finds in Catholicism, a corruption running all the way back to the origins of our faith. We must fall back on what she calls "the myth of return to origins" in order to make "a more radical interpretation of the revelatory paradigm to encompass contemporary experiences, while discarding institutions and traditions that contradict meaningful, just, and truthful life." In this fashion, feminists are able to "set the original tradition against its later corruption." She cites the Reformation as a precedent for this type of theology. (*Ibid.*, pp. 16–17.)
4. Thomas Hopko, "On the Male Character of the Christian Priesthood", in Hopko (ed.), *Women and the Priesthood*, pp. 101–102.
5. John Meyendorff, cited by Bishop Kallistos Ware, "Man, Woman and the Priesthood of Christ", in Hopko (ed.), *Women and the Priesthood*, p. 14.
6. Ruether, *Sexism and God-Talk*, pp. 140–141.
7. Elizabeth Schussler Fiorenza, *In Memory of Her* (New York: Crossroad Publishing Company, 1983), p. 269.
8. According to Fiorenza, for example, "the history of early Christianity is written from the perspective of the historical winners. For the most part, official Christian history and theology reflect those segments of the church which have undergone this patriarchalization process and theologically legitimated it with the formulation of the canon" (*Ibid.*, p. 83).
9. Rosemary Radford Ruether, "Meetings, But Not of Minds", in *National Catholic Reporter*, July 5, 1985.
10. Ruether is quite explicit about this in her book *Liberation Theology* (New York/Paramus/Toronto: Paulist Press, 1972), where she speaks of death as "a friend that completes the proper cycle of the human soul" (p. 125) and says of heaven that it is "not a supernatural 'place' to which one goes by abolishing the earth, but it is the mandate for what ought to be done on earth" (p. 56).
11. Ruether, "Meetings, But Not of Minds".
12. *Ibid.*
13. Belonick, "The Spirit of the Female Priesthood", p. 137.
14. *Ibid.*, pp. 137–138.
15. One notable exception is Fr. Donald J. Keefe, SJ, who has written several articles exploring a Christocentric and covenantal understanding of the revelation. Articles by him which pursue the relationship between the covenantal character of creation and the sacramental

character of the Church and of history include "Mary as Created Wisdom, The Splendor of the New Creation," *The Thomist* 47 (July 1983): 395-420, "The Sacrament of the Good Creation," *Faith & Reason* (Summer 1983): 128-141, and "Toward a Renewal of Sacramental Theology," *The Thomist* 44 (July 1980): 357-371. Mention should also be made of Gerald Emmett Cardinal Carter's "Do This in Memory of Me", a pastoral letter on the sacrament of priestly orders, issued on December 8, 1983, which very explicitly places priestly orders within a Trinitarian-based covenantal ecclesiology.

16. Donald J. Keefe, "Sacramental Sexuality and the Ordination of Women," *Communio* V (Fall 1978): 248-249.

17. Karl Stern, *The Flight from Woman* (New York: Farrar, Straus and Giroux, The Noonday Press, 1965), pp. 302-303.

18. Hans Urs von Balthasar, in the epilogue to Louis Bouyer, *Woman in the Church*, trans. by Marilyn Teichert (San Francisco: Ignatius Press, 1979), p. 113.

19. Walter J. Ong, *Fighting for Life: Contest, Sexuality, and Consciousness* (Ithaca/London: Cornell University Press, 1981), p. 98.

20. Cited by Stern, *Flight from Woman*, p. 215.

21. Bouyer, *Woman in the Church*, p. 102.

22. *Ibid.*, p. 98.

23. *Ibid.*, p. 73.

24. C.S. Lewis, in essay included in Bouyer, *Woman in the Church*, p. 130.

25. Stern, *Flight from Woman*, p. 273.

26. *Ibid.*, p. 274.

27. Rosemary Radford Ruether, "The Roman Catholic Story," in Rosemary Radford Ruether and Eleanor McLaughlin (eds), *Women of Spirit* (New York: Simon and Schuster, 1979), p. 382.

28. Ong, *Fighting for Life*, p. 101.

29. Adapted from an article which appeared in *Faith & Reason* Box 87 Front Royal, Virginia XIII,3 (1987). Reprinted with permission.

Women Elders?

Andrew T. B. McGowan

INTRODUCTION

As a minister of the Church of Scotland and an orthodox Calvinist, writing in a book Female Priesthood, the very first thing to be said is that I do not believe in any kind of priesthood, male or female! The only priesthood I recognize is that of Jesus Christ, our great High Priest. He has made one sacrifice which was accepted by God and which needs no repetition.[1]

Thus, in the Church of Scotland, as in most Reformed churches throughout the world, we have Ministers not priests, the Lord's Supper and not a Mass, a Communion Table and not an altar.[2]

So much for the Protestant polemic! But this does not mean that the issue of women's ordination has no bearing upon our situation. Quite the reverse. In fact it is a more radical issue for us because it impinges not only upon the ordination of what some call 'clergy' but also upon the ordination of what some call 'laity'. Let me explain.

Each congregation in the Church of Scotland has a Kirk Session which exercises pastoral care and oversight. Each Kirk Session is made up of a number of Elders with at least one Minister who acts as Moderator (chairman).[3]

The fact that the Minister is full-time, and has normally spent a minimum of six academic years in training, leads many people to regard him as a 'protestant Priest,' a clergyman among the laity. But this is not the case. We believe in the priesthood of all believers, and reject the distinction between clergy and laity.[4]

In the oversight of the congregation the Minister is equal in status to his fellow Elders. The only real distinction is that he has been set apart for the teaching ministry. What we call 'Ministers', then, are more properly designated 'Teaching Elders,' and what we call 'Elders' are 'Ruling Elders'.

Both Elders and Ministers are ordained,[5] and that ordination is for life (barring serious flaws in life or doctrine). We also have 'Deacons' (or 'Members of the Congregational Board') who are responsible for the practical, financial and fabric concerns of the church. These are not normally ordained.

A good case can be made for saying that our Presbyterian structures are based firmly on the New Testament.[6] In 1 Timothy 3 we have the distinction between elders and deacons, and in 1 Timothy 3:17 we have the distinction between an 'ordinary' elder and a 'teaching elder'.

There is no 'higher' office than an Elder. It is significant in this context that even Peter claimed to be an elder (1 Peter 5:1) not a priest or a bishop, far less a pope!

This description has of necessity been brief, and clearly there is much that has not been said. If I were setting out to state and defend the ecclesiology of Scottish Presbyterianism I would spend another twenty pages or so on the above material, but that is not my purpose here. My sole intention is to provide sufficient information to assist those who are unfamiliar with the Church of Scotland to understand something of what follows.

WOMEN ELDERS & MINISTERS

It was agreed at the General Assembly of the Church of Scotland in 1966 that Women could be ordained to the Eldership on the same terms and conditions as men. That was followed in 1968 by a decision to ordain women to the Ministry. There are no records kept of the number of congregations which have appointed women as Elders, but judging by the monthly list of new Elders (in which 'Mrs' and 'Miss' appear with astonishing frequency) there must only be a small minority of congregations which have not succumbed. The number of women Ministers, on the other hand, is still relatively small.

Ministers are ordained by the Moderator of Presbytery, on behalf of the Presbytery. Elders are ordained by the Minister of the Congregation in which the Elders are to serve, on behalf of the Kirk Session (which elects them).

PARTICIPATION IN WOMEN'S ORDINATION

This means that I, as a Minister, may be asked to participate in the ordination of women at two levels. First, as a member or as a Moderator of Presbytery I might be asked to take part in the ordination service of a woman Minister called or appointed to serve within the bounds of my Presbytery. Second, as a parish Minister I might be asked by my Kirk Session to ordain to the Eldership a woman whom they had elected to serve in this capacity.

Women as Ministers

The first level does not present insuperable problems. As a member of Presbytery, if I am asked to attend and participate ('lay on hands') at the ordination of a woman Minister, I can decline – without giving a reason.

It is undoubtedly possible, within the present law, for a Presbytery to proceed with disciplinary action against a member of Presbytery who refuses to participate in such an ordination, but it is unlikely that such action would be taken at this point in time. The Presbytery Clerk normally telephones people in advance to ask them to take part in ordinations and other special services before submitting names to the full meeting of Presbytery. Most Clerks, on discovering that someone had a problem with participation in the ordination of women, would simply telephone someone else.

As Moderator of Presbytery the situation is a little more difficult. I served as Moderator of the Presbytery of Lochaber several years ago (a Moderator, except in exceptional circumstances, serves for one year only) and during my year of office no woman was called to serve as a Minister within the bounds. If such a circumstance had arisen I would have asked my immediate predecessor to take the service, but Presbytery could have rejected this option and placed me in a difficult position.

There has been at least one case where a Minister agreed to become Moderator of a Presbytery only on condition that he would not be asked to take part in the ordination of a woman Minister, and received assurances on this point before accepting office. On the other hand, there is at least one senior and distinguished Minister who has never been invited to take the chair as Moderator of his Presbytery, partly because his views on this matter are known.

Women as Elders

The second level is much more difficult, and indeed is

the arena in which the major battles are taking place at present.[7]

As a Minister (and Moderator of the Kirk Session) I must ordain to the Eldership any woman who has been elected to that office by the Kirk Session. I have no right of veto, and no legal grounds for refusing to carry out the ordination (assuming that all the procedure has been carried out properly and that there is no objection to the life or doctrine of the woman concerned).

THE CASE AGAINST WOMEN'S ORDINATION

But why should I decline to participate in the ordination of a woman to the Eldership or Ministry?

For some people (perhaps including some of the contributors to this volume) opposition to women's ordination may be based on the authority of the church, the importance of tradition, the fact that Christ was a man, or whatever. But for me, opposition to the ordination of women is grounded solely upon the authority of the Bible.

I believe that the Bible is a revelation from God, that it is his inspired Word, and is the final authority on all matters for the Christian. In other words I stand firmly in the evangelical Protestant tradition.

There are two main strands of biblical teaching which are relevant to our subject:[8]
1. The relation between man and woman in the created order.
2. The teaching of the New Testament as to who may hold office in the church.

1. Man and Woman

It seems clear from Genesis 2:18–25, as interpreted by 1

Corinthians 11:2-16, that woman was made as a companion for man and in marriage is functionally subordinate to the man. The teaching of Paul in 1 Corinthians 11:3 is very significant, "Now I want you to realise that the head of every man is Christ, and the head of the woman is man, and the head of Christ is God."[9]

This is not diminished in any way by Paul's remark that "There is neither Jew not Greek, slave nor free, male nor female, for you are all one in Christ Jesus" (Galatians 3:28). In our standing before God men and women are equal, but in relation to one another there is functional subordination.[10]

We can illustrate this point by thinking about the relation between the Father and the Son in the godhead. The Father and the Son are equal in every respect but yet the Son is functionally subordinate to his Father. Jesus did not come to do his own will but the will of his Father and in one memorable instance in Gethsemane had to triumph over self-will in order to do the will of the Father and go to the Cross. There is no incompatibility between equality of nature and functional subordination.

All of this is underlined by Ephesians 5:22-33.[11] In that passage the wife is told to obey her husband and to submit to him in everything, and the husband is told to love his wife. This teaching about the wife submitting to her husband is echoed in Colossians 3:18-21; Titus 2:5; and 1 Peter 3:1-6.

For the Christian, marriage is not a convenient social custom which has evolved over the centuries but is rather part of the very fabric of the created order, the way God intended man and woman to live together. Thus the relation between man and woman in marriage is part of that creation ordinance.

Man and woman, then, are by nature equal. Nevertheless, there is within that equality a functional subordination, especially in marriage and, as we shall now see, in the church.

2. Teaching anent Office in the Church

In 1 Timothy 2:12 Paul says that he does not permit women to teach or to have authority over men.

Now if Paul had said that he did not permit women to teach or have authority *because* of the culture in which they lived; or *because* the time had not yet come for such a step, then there might have been an argument for saying that his prohibition was no longer valid, as many suggest today.

But Paul, in vv.13,14, makes it clear that his decision was neither cultural nor time-conditioned, but was based on a past event, at the time of the creation of man and woman. In other words, Paul says that women are forbidden to teach or to have authority over men *because* of what happened in the Garden of Eden.

By basing his prohibition on a past event, which by definition cannot be reversed, Paul is saying that the prohibition itself is irreversible.

Women, then, in the church as in marriage, are to be functionally subordinate to men and are not to teach or have authority.

An Elder must be apt to teach (1 Timothy 3:2) and a Minister (or Teaching Elder) devotes his whole energy to the task of teaching. Elders and Ministers together have authority or oversight in the Church. Women, therefore, may not be Elders or Ministers.[12]

RESPONSE

It seems to me that the above argument must be taken seriously, especially by evangelicals who accept the basic presupposition concerning the authority and inspiration of the Bible. And yet many arguments are raised against it.

The objections come in two main categories:

1. Those who do not accept that the Bible has the kind of authority which I ascribe to it, and who therefore feel able to disregard parts of its teaching while still claiming to be Christians. Such people may voice their objection to what the Bible says on this matter in a variety of ways:

a. The Bible is not a revelation from God, rather it is the record of the life and experience of the people of God through many generations. The culture of the people determined much of what the Bible says, and hence it has no continuing authority in a different culture.

b. The Bible is a revelation from God, but revelation is progressive. God was gradually teaching more and more as the generations passed. In the Old Testament we have a faint and unclear picture of God and his salvation. This is clearer in the New Testament. Today we have a still clearer picture. Therefore, much of what is in the Bible is neither valid nor acceptable today.

c. Paul was a man of God, but he was still a man, and hence much of what he writes is personal opinion which has no authority for us.

d. Paul was completely mistaken and unenlightened.

2. Those who accept the authority of the Bible but yet disagree with my interpretation as to how the teaching of the Bible relates to this particular subject. Such people might express one of the following opinions:

a. Paul's objection to women teaching or having authority over men was due to the peculiar situation in the church at that time. Just as he did not denounce slavery but gave teaching to the effect that slaves should respect and obey their masters, so in this area he accepted the situation as he found it and gave teaching accordingly. Nevertheless, his teaching that in Christ Jesus there is neither male nor female was destined ultimately to change the situation. Just as Paul would be delighted at the abolition of slavery so he would be delighted at the ordination of women.

b. There were, in the church at that time, certain women who misbehaved during public worship and were in danger of bringing the church into disrepute. Paul's prohibition was related to that specific situation.

c. The teaching of the Bible is not so clear-cut as the passage from 1 Timothy 2 would suggest. A complete analysis of all the passages in the Bible relating to women's ministry, including the story of Deborah (Judges 4 & 5); the story of Philip's daughters (Acts 21:9) and so on, leads to the conclusion that women's ministry is not prohibited.

The first set of objections I have to dismiss on the basis that we have no shared presupposition as to the nature of authority or criteria for decision-making. For me, the authority of the Bible is fundamental so that what the Bible says, God says. Those who do not share this view are, of course, entitled to their opinion, but we cannot properly debate or interact since we base our arguments on different foundations. I regard them as mistaken, and they regard me as a fundamentalist! We would have to discuss the authority of the Bible before we could debate women's ordination or any other matters.

The second set of objections I take very seriously, although I disagree with their conclusions.

On (a) we must question whether Paul was simply accepting the current situation in society, or whether indeed, as I believe, he was explaining a creation ordinance.

On (b) I would have to argue that the situation presupposed as a means of exegesis is purely hypothetical with little or no evidence to support it. It is a convenient rather than a convincing interpretation of the textual evidence.

On (c) I would respond by saying that the evidence for an alternative exegesis, namely, that women may be teachers or have authority over men, is unconvincing.

Having said this, however, I must say that I respect the views of my brothers and sisters in Christ whose position is in some way represented by the second set of objections. If someone genuinely believes that the Bible permits the ordination of women then I disagree but respect their integrity.

COMPROMISE

The position with which I have no sympathy at all is the position taken by some of my fellow-evangelicals who argue that women's ordination is forbidden by the Bible but that we should nevetheless be prepared to participate in such ordinations in order to remain within the denomination. This view is perhaps the most generally-held position among evangelicals in the Church of Scotland today.

A recent outbreak of this debate was prompted by a letter written to the Church of Scotland magazine 'Life and Work' by the Rev. Dr. Nigel M. de S. Cameron [13], warden of Rutherford House, an evangelical centre for study and research in Edinburgh. As a member of the Council of Rutherford House I had a particular interest in what our warden had to say.

Dr Cameron was writing about the case of a Minister, the Rev. Iain Wright, who had been instructed by his Presbytery to ordain a woman to the Eldership. Mr Wright had refused to do this and an appeal to a higher court (Synod) was pending. Dr Cameron said that he was opposed to the ordination of women on biblical-theological and on practical grounds, but he then went on to say this,

"But we nevertheless exhort our colleagues to accept the decisions of the Church and to obey its law, since we do not find the ordination of women a *casus belli* that could justify schism."

His subsequent appeal to the Church of Scotland authorities to find some means of avoiding confrontation on this issue, his comment that many of the "finest young ministers in the church" are prepared to take a stand against the present law of the church, and his reminder that those of us who are opposed to the ordination of women stand in the broad stream of Christendom, do not make his unfortunate words quoted above any easier to bear.

Quite simply, Dr Cameron is saying that we should disobey the voice of God speaking in the Bible for ecclesiastical reasons. In other words, we should deliberately ignore our consciences and participate in the ordination of women.

A response to Dr Cameron came very quickly from the Rev. Professor Donald MacLeod, writing in the 'Monthly Record' of the Free Church of Scotland. He describes Dr Cameron's position and then says,

"He asks Mr Wright to do what he knows to be wrong, simply because it is commanded by the General Assembly. We must obey men rather than God. There are many words for such a course of action. Evangelical is not one of them."[14]

Many of us in the Church of Scotland, although we stand side by side with Dr Cameron on many issues, are in complete agreement with Donald MacLeod's assessment of the situation.

And so among the evangelicals in the Church of Scotland who are opposed in principle to the ordination of women there are these two camps.

First, there are those who, like Dr Cameron, believe that this is not a fundamental issue, not an issue which should be allowed to tear the Church apart. Such people believe that the long-term strategy of reforming the church by means of prayer and a systematic expository ministry of God's Word is more important than any short-term compromise which might be necessary in order to achieve this end. They are prepared to speak out against the ordination of women, and to vote accordingly in the courts of the church, but in the last analysis they take the view that our position within the denomination must not be sacrificed on the altar of this issue.

Second, there are those who, like myself, believe that such a compromise is unacceptable. We agree that the ordination of women is not a fundamental of the faith, but our argument remains that the authority of the Bible *is* a fundamental of the faith - and it is the authority of the Bible which is at stake here.

Those of us who take this latter position are unwilling to break with the Church of Scotland. We do not see why we should leave our denomination when we are in complete agreement with both the standard (Scripture) and principal subordinate standard (The Westminster Confession of Faith) of the church's doctrine.

In short, we will not do what the Bible and our conscience forbids, and we will not 'go quietly'. It is our conviction that the Church of Scotland has departed from the truth of God's Word, and we feel that we must say so, despite any action which may be taken against us.

The evangelicals who are opposed to women's ordination, being thus divided into two camps, have failed to speak with the united and co-ordinated voice which one might have hope for, and hence there is a very real danger of us being 'picked off' one at a time. Indeed this is already happening.[15]

THE FUTURE

There are basically two possible scenarios as we look to the future:

1. Confrontation

One possibility is that the Church of Scotland will begin to increase the pressure on those of us who will not participate in the ordination of women. In some cases that would be relatively easy, for example, where the Minister does not have substantial support for his views within his own Kirk Session. In other cases, where Minister and Kirk Session have a substantial measure of agreement on this issue, it would be more difficult, but by no means impossible.

It is, then, not inconceivable that at some point in the not too distant future those of us who find ourselves unable and unwilling to compromise on this matter might be forced out of the denomination.

2. Modus Vivendi

The other possibility is that some *modus vivendi* will be found to enable us to remain within the denomination. Some effort has recently been made at quite a high level to find a way out of this dilemma which will not involve disciplinary action or deposition, and these efforts might well succeed. After all, the Church of Scotland cannot afford to lose Ministers! At the moment there are about 1,250 parish Ministers (apart from those serving in the offices, colleges, schools etc.). Statistics show that in the year 2000 there will only be about 800 Ministers available for this parish work! With the additional problem of a serious financial crisis there are many senior figures in the establishment who do not agree with our position but who will do what they can to avoid losing Ministers (and congregations) at this difficult juncture.

But what kind of *modus vivendi* would be possible? Various suggestions have been mooted:

a. If a Kirk Session elects a woman to the Eldership and the Minister of that congregation will not take part in the ordination, then another Minister might be invited to take his place at the service of ordination.

b. The ordination of Elders, like the ordination of Ministers, could be carried out by Presbyteries instead of at a local level - as in the Presbyterian Church of Ireland.

c. Certain congregations who do not want women Elders might be granted permission to retain that status. Ministers who are opposed to the ordination of women could then serve in these congregations.

d. Congregations could be instructed to ask a Minister his views on the ordination of women when being interviewed by the 'Vacancy Committee'. If that congregation then elected a Minister who had stated his opposition to women's ordination then they would be obliged to respect his conscience and not ordain any women to the Eldership during his incumbency.

I am deeply unhappy with (a) because it is rather like Pilate who washed his hands while ensuring that the deed was done! The option of (b) is undesirable although it would put the situation anent women Elders on a par with the position of women Ministers. If (c) were adopted I fear that gradually the 'remnant' would be reduced to a handful of congregations, mostly north and west of the highland line.

To a certain extent option (d) already exists, although not in a legal sense. My own situation is an example of an 'unofficial' use of option (d).

In July of last year I finished a short-term appointment and was considering my future. When a congregation has no Minister they set up a vacancy committee. The task of this vacancy committee is to search for a replacement. The end result of their search is to appoint someone as 'Sole Nominee'. This nominee preaches before the whole congregation who then vote for or against. If the congregation votes in favour of the said nominee then a call is issued. If that call is sustained by the Presbytery within whose bounds the congregation lies then the Minister in question is inducted as Minister of the congregation.

In practice, when a Minister is invited to be 'Sole Nominee' it is more or less an invitation to become Minister. It is extremely rare for a congregation to turn down the choice of its own committee, and even rarer for Presbytery to refuse to sustain the call. I have never known of either situation.

Two congregations invited me to be Sole Nominee. In both cases the issue of women's ordination to the Eldership was raised. In the case of Church A it was raised by the committee, and in the case of Church B it was raised by me. The ensuing discussions were most interesting.

Church A already had one woman Elder, and they clearly had no theological or other problems with this. But yet they were prepared to have me as their Minister. Their argument went something like this: some of us are inclined to agree with your position, most of us are not. But if you were to come as our Minister we would respect your conscience and would not ask you to ordain a woman.

Church B had no women Elders and it seemed that they did not want any. Theologically they were at one with me on this, as on other matters. I nevertheless felt it necessary to say to them that I would not be prepared to ordain a woman to the Eldership. They fully understood and accepted my position.

I am now Minister of Church B!

It has to be said, however, that my 'Gentlemen's Agreement' with my new congregation has no legal standing whatsoever. If my Kirk Session decided tomorrow to elect a woman to the Eldership I would have no redress. I am convinced that this will not happen, but this conviction is based on a shared theological stance rather than on a legal agreement.

CONCLUSION

We now face a situation in the Church of Scotland where conscience is permitted on matters of doctrine, but not on matters of practice and procedure (or Church Law). Thus it is perfectly possible to deny the truth of the Incarnation, Resurrection and Ascension – to say nothing of the other biblical miracles – and yet remain a Minister of the Church of Scotland in good standing. Another Minister, however, who might be completely orthodox in every aspect of his theology, risks deposition from the Ministry because he will not ordain a woman to the Eldership, or participate in the ordination of a woman Minister.

NOTES

1. The Epistle to the Hebrews chapters 7-10.
2. For a history of the Church of Scotland see: J.H.S. Burleigh *A Church History of Scotland* (O.U.P. 1960).
3. For a complete description of the structures and 'law' of the Church of Scotland see, D.F.M. Macdonald (ed) *Practice and Procedure in The Church of Scotland* 6th Edition (The Committee on General Administration, The Church of Scotland, 1976).
4. In theory at least! Many Ministers do, however, regard themselves as 'clergy' and are happy for their congregations to do so also.
5. One anomaly is that an ordained Elder who becomes a Minister is re-ordained. Recently several Elders in the Irish Presbyterian Church who had just completed theological training asked that their first ordination be recognised as sufficient. This was turned down. They must be re-ordained.
6. See, for example, John Murray 'Office in the Church' in *Collected Writings of John Murray* (Banner of Truth, 1977) Vol. 2, pp. 357-365.
7. See the symposium *Women Elders in the Kirk?* A.T.B. McGowan (ed) which is to be published by Christian Focus Publications early in 1990 (ISBN 1 871676 30 4).
8. Both of these areas are dealt with thoroughly by Susan T. Foh in *Women & the Word of God: A Response to Biblical Feminism* (Presbyterian & Reformed, 1979).
9. On 1 Corinthians 11 see C. Hodge *1 & 2 Corinthians* (Banner of Truth, 1974) and G.H. Clark 1 Corinthians (Presbyterian & Reformed, 1975).
10. Calvin makes this point in his commentary on 1 Corinthians (Edited by D.W. and T.F. Torrance, Eerdmans, 1960) p. 229.
11. William Hendriksen's commentary on Ephesians (Banner of Truth, 1972) gives a firm yet balanced exegesis of this passage.
12. For a fuller analysis of the various passages of scripture which are relevant to the debate see the article by Peter White in the aforementioned symposium *Women Elders in the Kirk?*13. February 1989 issue.
14. March 1989 issue.
15. See my own article in *Women Elders in the Kirk?* for a description of the Iain Wright case mentioned above, and various other contemporary cases.

Andrew T.B. McGowan
Minister of the Church of Scotland
Parish of Glasgow: Trinity Possil & Henry Drummond

Man, Woman
and Priesthood

James Tolhurst

An editorial in the Jesuit magazine *The Month*, said of the Declaration by the Vatican on the admission of women to the priesthood that it was "only as good as its theology".[1] This rather cavalier dismissal of a closely argued statement was not redeemed by a totally worked-out theology from the opposite point of view. Twenty years later, during which much heat and less light has been generated, it seems, in the light of recent developments an opportune time to examine the theology which argues that women cannot be admitted to the priesthood.

A Time of Emancipation

Many developments take place as a result of a slow, protracted evolution. But this has not been the case with regard to woman's emancipation. The struggle for emancipation, with its equally vehement resistance from within the corridors of power, has defined the nature of feminism. It has come to see itself as emerging from exploitation and repression. Pope John, in 1963 remarked "Far from being content with a purely passive role, . . . they are demanding both in domestic and in public life the rights and duties which belong to them as human persons".₂ This struggle is characterized by a clear desire for equality, and for the right of entry into all professions. It would appear to be accompanied by some unexamined assumptions, as made manifest by the fact that there is no clear – let alone rigorous – consideration of what feminity is. Vatican II talks of women fully playing their part "according to their own particular nature"₃ but leaves the rest unsaid.

Although I do not want to trespass on Mary Kenny's preserve, there is a strong current of opinion which says that the question of the priestly ministry of women is not dogmatic, but psychologico-pastoral.₄ Part of this is due to the possibly unseen influence of a philosophy expressed eloquently by Simone de Beauvoir which declares "One does not arrive in the world as woman, but one becomes a woman. No biological, mental or economic fate determines the form that a female human being takes on in the womb of society."₅ It is a small step to argue that "the service at the altar [is] not tied to being a man. Even more important, as a purely male function, lacking the female side, it is not wholly human and therefore remains incomplete".₆ The Movement for the Rights of Women in the Church (AKR) has put forward a demand that "a certain presence of women should be achieved in the ecclesiastical office, *so that a fully human form* of the office is rendered possible".₇

But the differentiation between men and women is not simply a matter of cultural programming which in time will eliminate all differences. Walter Kasper rightly says that "the human person only exists in the 'dual version' of man and woman. A woman is thus a person in her own specific way by being a woman. She is no less a person than a man is, but she is a person in her own way."₈

The problem about arguing as Greeley does that in God "feminine and masculine traits are blended in equal proportions"[9] is that in one sense it is perfectly true, because all that is best in humanity is to be found in the Creator, but at the same time it risks making God a combination of contrary characteristics. C G Jung who put forward the argument in detail can be said to have constructed "the most important Gnosticism of our century" for this very reason.[10]

At the same time, there is a slightly uncertain response from within the Church. Although Pope Paul stated that "women do not receive the call to the apostolate of the twelve and to the ordained ministry [and] we cannot change what our Lord did"[11], this only served to fuel the argument. People continued to claim that there were no theological objections to the possibility of women priests and pointed to the earlier admission of Teresa of Avila and Catherine of Sienna as Doctors of the Church. The Pope had, at the time made clear that "women were not meant to hold ministerial or magisterial office in the Church"[12] but attention had already been directed to the widespread encouragement of women special ministers of the Eucharist. In the midst of the debate about female altar servers (which, if allowed, would certainly not help the case)[13] opponents of the Church's position argue, albeit unfairly that the authorities are tacitly conceding what they cannot openly admit.

He Made Them Male and Female

But we must also realise that the confusion is stoked by those who maintain the position of the Koran that "men have authority over women because Allah has made the one superior to the other"[14]. Although this stance has often been repudiated by theologians[15], many will recall that there remained the argument that the wife was bound to give way to her husband's demands in marriage however unreasonable. Any theology which argues for a true role for women has to abandon this kind of sexual discrimination.[16] For although some men are 'softer' and some women 'harder', most are agreed that there are identifiable masculine and feminine qualities.

The very fact that we can identify characteristics which endure through the centuries argues a substratum which is not interchangeable. Lehman underlines this when he states that "beyond sexual characteristics and functions, there is biological-psychological evidence for a substantial difference between the sexes which cannot reduce to socially enforced or historico-culturally developed 'roles' "[17] Rather, we should speak of a "social stylization of genetic dispositions"[18] because culture builds on the differentiation that is already there.

When he considered the whole topic, the late C S Lewis, who made a foray into the subject in *Perelandra*[19] said that "one of the ends for which sex was created was to symbolize to us the hidden things of God"[20] We cannot simply divorce the division of the sexes from the background we are given in Genesis. When Christ was asked by the Pharisees about the question of divorce he pointed out that God who had made them in the beginning had made them male and female and through marriage they were enabled to recover that one-ness out of which male and female had been created.[21]

It cannot therefore be a question of some neuter creation in which identities are fused. Margaret Mead has already reminded us that far from expressing humanity, "every adjustment that minimizes a difference, a vulnerability, in one sex, a differential strength in the other, diminishes their possibility of complementing each other, and . . . leads to a duller vision of human life in which each is denied the fullness of humanity that each might have had."[22]

With Christ in View

When we approach the Old Testament we identify not only the concept of a transcendent God but also the clear image of Fatherhood. The relationship of Israel to Yahweh is that of Son to father, clay to potter: "O Lord, you are our Father; we are the clay and you are our potter; we are all the work of your hand" (Is 63: 15-16; cf Jer 31:9). The Lord is the father who protects, like a shepherd, but also like a lion who sees his sons trembling (Hos 11:10). It is to him that Israel can turn because he is the Father of the orphan, defender of the widow . . . who leads the prisoners forth . . . at the head of your people" (Ps 68:5ff). He provides that strength because Israel can say "You are my Father, my God the rock of my salvation" (Ps 89:26).

It can be argued that God is also compared to a mother who, even if a woman abandons her child, will not forget Israel (Is 49:15). But even here we notice that God is the Mighty One of Jacob, who lifts up his hand to the nations and raises his signal to the peoples, who dispossesses the King of Babylon (Is 49:22.26).[23]

The relationship both of rock and of son is not accidental to the person of the Messiah, nor is that of shepherd. If God calls Israel, his Son out of Egypt (Hos 11:1) it is because it looks towards that time when his Anointed will also be called to lead his people into the new Promised Land where he will be their shepherd.

Salvation history is not divided into two stages, but is one continuous account which unfolds like a tapestry. The whole extent of the panorama only becomes clear in the latter stages, but no re-weaving has to be done.

It is quite possible to add layers to the masculine symbolism of God so that the image of Kingship can be seen not as a despot but as a leader and saviour. But you cannot eliminate the whole concept in the same way that you cannot re-write the *Our Father* as *Our Mother*. We can see a certain congruity in the Messiah being a man when he came into the world, since he fulfills in himself that quality which was associated with God, as shepherd and as Lord. It was that relationship which so disconcerted the Pharisees when they were asked: "How is it that David, inspired by the Spirit, calls him Lord . . . If David thus calls him Lord, how is he his son?" (Mt 22:43ff)

There is a strong theme in the Fathers which sees Christ as the key to understanding the creation of man. Tertullian states "Whatever was the form and expression that was then given to the clay by the creator, Christ was in his thoughts as one day to become man."[24] It is this same perspective which Pope John Paul puts forward when he says that "the eternal truth about the human being, man and woman—a truth which is immutably fixed in human experience—at the same time constitutes the mystery which only in the Incarnate Word takes on light since Christ freely reveals man to himself."[25] But is it possible also to argue to some organic connection between the advent of Christ as male and the division of "Adam" into male and female? If it is something more than a matter of biological convenience, argues Holloway[26] then we must see it as linked with the need for Christ to come into the world as its Lord, and for the world to receive him and for a Womb to be determined for him.

In this perspective, the greeting of Adam to Eve "Here at last is bone of my bones and flesh of my flesh" (Gen 2:23) has a deeper significance because it includes the voice of the Second Adam as he comes into contact with the womb that receives him. The feminine principle receives him as Lord and is in turn determined by him: "for nowhere does he take hold of the angels, but of the seed of Abraham he takes hold" (Heb 2:16). So the power of the life in the human species must be divided into the principle that takes hold and determines, and the principle which receives and responds and is determined. Christ who is to come must be the determiner since he is the Uncreated who must determine the womb of woman in Mary, and so must come as masculine to determine that life which was made flesh and lived among us. By virtue of being, when he comes as man, Christ must come as male.

It is strange that Rahner could assert that "the maleness of Jesus was nothing but a presupposition for accomplishing his task without real significance to salvation and indifferent as far as God's self-disclosure is concerned."[27] Surely we are dealing with Wisdom, *Logic* itself, so although in principle God might have acted differently, we ought to assume that his becoming man is very definitely part of God's self disclosure as St Anselm argued in *Cur Deus Homo?* One has the slight suspicion that in Rahner there are deeper doubts at work which question the very nature of God but this itself is not a subject that can be adequately dealt with here.[28] The scandal of particularity attached to God's revelation in Christ, to which McDade refers[29] is far easier to grasp, even though it remains a scandal if we see the maleness of Jesus as part of the reasoning behind the division of the sexes into male and female at the beginning of creation.

"The Head of the Woman is the Man"

The Pauline texts have been brought into play on both sides of the argument and they will be discussed elsewhere in this book.

Many theologians, like Küng, take the view that "the New Testament should be viewed as a time-conditioned work" and instance the veiled women of Corinth.[30] Others have commented on the command to keep silence (I Tim 2:12). These are then set alongside the revolutionary statement "In Christ Jesus there is no distinction of Jew or Greek, slave or free citizen, male or female" (Gal 3:28), which it is said abolishes any objection to a female priesthood. But surely we are talking on different levels. In Christ there is complete equality of dignity but at the same time there is a distinction in the sexual order for *the purpose of ministry*. This is the crucial meaning of Paul's "I would have you know that the head of every man is Christ; and the head of the woman is the man and the head of Christ is God" (I Cor 11:3). We cannot set that against Galatians 3 but must take it together with Paul's comments on the unique vocation which man and woman enjoy in Christ. At the same time we have to realise the truth of his words which underlies in fact the prohibition of women preaching and the command that they should be veiled. The headship of the man cannot be interpreted as bestowing dominion over the woman because both have been given dominion in the beginning (cf Gen 1:28ff). St Peter is quite clear when he says that husband and wife "are joint heirs of the grace of life" (I Pet 3:7). That does not mean we must dismiss the other concept but rather investigate the argument which says that "the man" derives his status as "head of her flesh" from the relationship of his sexuality to the flesh of Christ as Head; and "the woman" from her relationship to the Church which is Christ's Body (cf Eph 5:21ff).

The male must exist and show in his sexuality the promise of Christ and the headship which is his as Head of the Human Race, in his ministerial role. "He is that Christ figure in as much," says Holloway, "as the womb is made to be prompted to life by him"[31]. But conversely, the woman, through her womb, is creation's gift to God for the purpose of Christ. In that sense she is *subject*. It is however a "subjection" to the Father for the purposes of Christ for as Pope John Paul has said "In God's eternal plan, woman is the one in whom the order of love in the created world of persons takes first root."[32] In her "subjection" the whole of Creation gives of its own to God for the flesh of God made man. Both man and woman therefore together make up that total Christ of which the Letter to the Ephesians speaks.

It can further be argued of course that we can only fully understand this "subjection" if we appreciate the unique vocation of the Woman as seen in Revelations chapter 12. *Mulieris Dignitatem* talks of her as of cosmic scale[33] and we can see that she is both Mother earth, clothed with the sun and crowned with stars, and the womb of the Virgin Mary, and in her also the Church. In Mary we have the perfect exemplar of the ministry of woman through whom the Church itself comes into being. Humanity cannot provide of its own, it must wait upon the determination of God, but Woman can, and one Woman has provided the means by which Christ comes into the world, and in this way Mary is blessed among women. (Lk 1:42)

It is going to be impossible to live and believe in such a theology without an appreciation of the complementarity of man and woman in married life.

There must be a working out of the ministerial role in practice.

The concept of "equal but different" was echoed even in Pius XI's encyclical letter *Casti Conubii* (1930) which noted that "there is a true equality between them, which is to be recognized in all that pertains to the person and dignity of a human being, and in all that is implied by the marriage contract and is inherent in wedlock itself". But also "there must be a certain inequality and adjustment, demanded by the welfare of the family and by the unity and ordered stability which must reign in the home".[34] The Pope feared that neglect of such a distinction would result in enslavement by the husband; instead, there has been enslavement by the demands of the independent feminine role itself.[35] It is essential to preserve in woman that capacity for femininity: "the fact that she is a human person, and, at the same time, this particular person, by the fact of her femininity"[35]. There must be a concerted attempt to recognize the right of women to have a role in society which is not just a copy of the male role, but one which is unique. Gorbachov has written "We have discovered that many of our problems—in children's and young people's behaviour, in our morals, culture and in production—are partially caused by the weakening of family ties and slack attitude to family responsibilities. This is a paradoxical result of our sincere and politically justified desire to make women equal with men in everything. Now, in the course of perestroika, we have begun to overcome this shortcoming".[37] At virtually the same moment Pope John Paul II was telling the workers of Lodz that "the true advancement of women demands of society a particular recognition of maternal and family responsibilities because they constitute a value *superior* to all other public tasks and professions"[38] It is not patronizing women to want them to be women with all the warmth and tenderness and priority as mothers and ministers of life which only they can give to family life.

The Christian Priesthood

The argument for the differentiation of the sexes and the necessity of the maleness of Christ needs to be seen not simply as a fully logical decision of divine omnipotence but because of "an essential orientation built into the mystery of the Incarnation".[39]

This would argue that when the Word was made flesh he must be male and also he must be priest: "When Christ came into the world, he said, 'Sacrifices and offerings you have not desired, but a body you have prepared for me . . . and by that will we have been sanctified through the offering of the body of Jesus Christ once and for all'" (Heb 10:5.10). Christ's priesthood is rooted in his being Son of Man.

It is unfortunate that much of the argument for the admission of women to the priesthood revolves around the abolition of discrimination. Küng argues that there are no serious theological reasons against the ordination of women but that this comes about because of traditional views about women's sinfulness, and her being created second, which cannot be traced to Christ but are part of "a radical theological defamation" against women[40]. In similar vein Schillebeeckx says "that this is a purely historically conditioned cultural pattern, understandable in antiquity and even until recently, but problematical in a changed culture which is aware of real discrimination against women"[41]. These arguments themselves suffer from the defect that they are looking backwards with contemporary trends very much in mind.

There is no doubt that certain women claim a right to be ordained, and this has been identified by the Anglican Report when it says "women claim it and congregations affirm the call". But the Report continues: "what questions does contemporary experience pose in respect of the tradition?"[42] The idea of *reception* has been put forward but in the Roman Catholic sense such a popular consensus must be recognized and adjudged by the authority of the Church not vice versa.

The Pontifical Biblical Commission when discussing the matter could not find any proof that ordained ministry had been exercised by woman at the time of the New Testament[43]. There is no doubt that there were female priesthoods for instance in the cult of Isis, in the worship of Dionysius, Artemis and Demeter but not in Christian circles. Although the Canon Law Society of America argued that there did seem to be a real ordination of women in the early centuries,[44] Agnes Cunningham, who delivered a keynote speech to the Catholic Theological Society on the role of women, found that "extant evidences for this practice are limited" and "the admission of women to ordination in any one or in several particular Churches does not seem to have prevailed in continuity over an extended period of time".[45] It is this argument from a sustained tradition and not from isolated sources which is very telling and this was substantially the conclusion of the Episcopal Commission of the American bishops.[46] In a more cautious vein, the editorial in the Jesuit periodical *The Month* says "it is impossible to prove that Jesus' choice of men as apostles was inspired by social and cultural reasons alone."[47]

The Witness of the Early Church

Moreover, there is the fact that women were totally excluded from the office of priest and levite. All authoritative commentators agree on this.[48] It is not true that there is an argument from silence because Epiphanius, Irenaeus, Tertullian and Augustine express severe disapproval. So also does Firmilian of Caesarea in a letter to St Cyprian, and St John Chrysostom, who states that women are excluded from the ministry by divine law.[49] The Bishop of Salamis mentions the liturgical aberrations of the Collyridian women of Armenia who sacrificed in honour of Our Lady: "It is reported that certain women there in Arabia (i.e. east of Palestine) have introduced this absurd teaching from Thrace: how they offer up a sacrifice of bread rolls in the name of the Ever Virginal and hold their meetings in that very name, and how they undertake something that far exceeds proper measure in the name of the Holy Virgin. In an unlawful and blasphemous ceremony, they ordain women, through whom they offer up the sacrifice in the name of Mary. This means that the entire proceeding is godless and sacrilegious, a perversion of the message of the Holy Spirit; in fact, the whole thing is diabolical and a teaching of the impure spirit".[50]

It is significant that when heretical sects [like the modern Gnostics of the West Coast] did ordain women, the Church from the earliest times inveighed against it as we can gauge from the Apostolic Constitutions which state "we do not allow women to teach [so] how can anyone agree that they—in contempt of their nature—should assume the office of priest? For it is ignorant heathen ungodliness that leads to the ordination of priestesses for female deities, but not the command of Christ".[51] In the same vein Pope Gelasius in 494: "As we have noted with vexation, contempt for divine truths has reached such a level that even women, it is reported, serve at holy altars; and everything that is entrusted exclusively to the service of men is performed by the sex that has no right to do so."[52] Instead of seeing this as a typical male reaction, we might reflect that it reveals the righteous indignation against the incursions of unsavoury heresy at the heart of what was most solemn—namely the Holy Mysteries themselves.

It would seem that in those days, as well as now, there were not lacking groups who flouted the received teaching of the Church. There is no clear evidence that the Church ever gave way either over a long period or universally throughout its dominions. The admission of women deaconesses has been examined by Martimort. His conclusion was that "a deaconess in the Byzantine rite was in no wise a female deacon. She exercised a totally different ministry from that of the deacons."[53] We need to distinguish the very real *jurisdiction* exercised by women, from *ordination*. The Abbess of Las Huelgas near Burgos, up until 1870 described herself as "Lady, superior, prelate, legitimate administrator of the spiritual and temporal matters of the said royal monastery . . . as well as the convents, churches, hermitages affiliated with it, and the villages and places of its jurisdiction, manors and vassalages, in virtue of the apostolic bull and concessions with a jurisdiction that is plenary, privative, quasi-episcopal, nullius diocesis, and with royal privileges, a double jurisdiction which we exercise in peaceful possession as is publicly well known . . . The power to act judicially, just as the Lord bishops, in criminal, civil, criminal and beneficial cases, to grant dismissorial letters for ordination, faculties to preach, confess, exercise the care of souls, enter into religion, the power to confirm abbesses, to issue censures, and finally to convoke a synod".54 It recalls the rather grandiose titles given to themselves by *episcopi vagantes* as charted by the late Peter Anson. These 'mitred dowagers', because of their proximity to the court could and did lord it over the locals, but there is no suggestion that they possessed ordination. Innocent III's letter to the local Spanish bishops, pointing out that the keys of the kingdom had been given to the apostles and not to Mary has been interpreted as a reprimand to the abbesses of Las Huelgas.55

The evidence seems patchy at most and in no ways could be said to constitute a firm practice within the Church which appears to have strongly resisted the outbreaks where they occurred. Far from being a matter that could be decided on the basis of sociology it seems more certain to conclude that the absence of clear evidence in support is a clear indication why "the Catholic Church has never felt that priestly or episcopal ordination can be conferred on women".56

The argument in favour of an exclusively male priesthood was put cogently by its supporters in the Anglican synodical report: "An all male priesthood will witness to those things about the nature of God which were signified in the particularity of Jesus' maleness: a male priesthood will continue most faithfully to represent the priesthood of Christ in the sacramental life of the Church."57 What we are dealing with is a priesthood according to the traditional understanding of the word. Brown is quite right when he says that the admission of women "would probably cause little difficulty in a Catholic community that no longer thinks of its clergy as priests".58 When the first woman, Antoinette Brown was ordained to the congregational

ministry in the United States in 1853, the Weslyan
Methodist, Luther Lee, in his ordination sermon
preached on the text from Galatians 3:28, arguing in
favour of a charismatic view of ministry. He understood preaching as a gift of the Spirit, an outpouring
of the Spirit at Pentecost, and argued that since
prophecy was clearly given by Christ to both men
and women, the Church could not exclude women
from the ministry.[59] Many Christians believe that the
priesthood is not primarily cultic but charismatic and
is the order of those who have received the Spirit,
but the result of this broad approach has been to
reduce the Sacrament of Orders to a delegation
inferior to the gift of the Spirit. In Pentecostalism
this reduces the ministry to the role of prophetic
elder—a fact which has not escaped the more discerning in the Charismatic movement. Sullivan is
right in stating that "for some the role of the
community is simply to recognise and confirm the
charismatic gifts by which the Holy Spirit designates
certain persons for ministry"[60]. But others on the
Evangelical side would also say that the sacrament
of Orders should be considered as a ministry of
the word because there is no particular sacramental
relationship and "the distinctive nature of the ordained ministry, according to the New Testament, is
surely pastoral oversight, which is mainly exercised
by the ministry of the word to which the ministry
of the sacraments also belong"[61]. We must not ignore
that such interpretations are firmly rooted in the
reformed consciousness and to a certain extent explain why it is possible for joint statements to
consider the ministry of women on the basis of
"the comprehensiveness of ministry"[62].

The Sign of the Priest

The Theology of the sacraments especially as seen in Bonaventure and St Thomas reinforces the argument for the maleness of the priest. Bonaventure says that "the person who is consecrated signifies Christ as Mediator; and since the mediator belonged to the male sex and can be signified only by the male sex, the capacity for receiving ordination is therefore appropriate only for men, who alone can represent Christ by nature and can bear the sign of the ordained character conformably with its reception".[63] The argument is in fact about the way in which a priest must reflect Christ the Priest in the likeness of being a person, and in no way undermines the equality of man and woman. It is further developed by St Thomas who takes up the point of *subjection* (status subiectionis) in reference to the man being the "head" of the wife: "Now, as a state of authority (eminentia gradus) cannot be signified in the female sex, since the state of subjection is inherent in that sex, it cannot, therefore receive the Sacrament of Ordination".[64] People may smile at the terminology but the point at issue is the correspondence demanded between the two ends of the equation: the relationship of Christ to the Church. A woman because she is not the "head" cannot signify Christ the Priest in this equation.[65]

The Pontifical Biblical Commission considering the function of baptising which they concede to women (in spite of the fact that deaconesses only anointed women in most cases) asked whether the Eucharist could also be opened to women along with the Sacrament of Reconciliation?[66] They did not seem to be aware that it is precisely these sacraments which constitute the priesthood as distinct from a ministry. For such, more than the common priesthood of the baptised is required.

We need to believe in something beyond a merely 'representative' function of the priesthood. There seems to be an over-use of Paul's words "so we are ambassadors for Christ, God making his appeal through us" (2 Cor 5:20) applying it to the priesthood. The editorial in *The Month* says that "it is not, however, Christian belief that the priest at the altar *impersonates* Jesus of Nazareth; rather, he *represents* our redeemer in celebrating the sacrament of our redemption"[67]. Impersonation of course has a pejorative connotation ("for purpose of entertainment or fraud"—OED) but it can also mean represent in bodily form. Does the editor exclude that? Lampe obviously does, because he says that "the ambassador represents the Queen . . . He is not a representation of the Queen. He does not impersonate her"[68]. If we follow the Bishop of Salisbury we seem to be faced with a ministry which passively allows the sacrifice to take place: "Everything is done by God the holy Trinity; and above all the sacrifice is performed totally by Christ, because it is his self-offering on Calvary to his Father which is made present to us—not anything we do". He further emphasises this by saying that any iconic theory "runs the risk of suggesting that Christ is present and active in the eucharistic minister in a unique mode and degree, an idea for which there is no basis in the general doctrine of grace or in specific authoritative teaching"[69]. There is sufficient basis in the teaching of the Fathers however, as for instance, St Cyprian who says "the priest truly acts in the place of Christ"[70]. The dilemma is closely mirrored in ARCIC I's statement in 1973 that "the action of the presiding minister . . . is seen to stand in a sacramental relation to what Christ himself did in offering his own sacrifice"[71]. This leaves open both a Catholic and an Evangelical interpretation but there is strong theological support for the argument that the priest does not act in his own name but in the person of Christ, the principal minister in every sacrament. St Thomas goes so far as to say "The priest enacts the image of Christ, in whose person and by whose power he pronounces the words of consecration"[72]. "The priest then, is the same" says Pius XII "Christ Jesus, whose sacred person is represented by His minister"[73]. Although the theology of the *character* still needs deeper theological investigation, it points to an interpenetration in the matter of Orders between the priest and Christ, so that in a sense, acting ministerially the priest is identified not just by analogy but "in a unique mode and degree" through a real participation ministerially through his own human nature in the priestly acts of Christ the Priest. The priest allows the being and the power of Christ, not his own power to work through him. This is especially true at the moment of transubstantiation, but also when with the fulness of the priesthood he speaks in solemn definition. We are not talking merely in metaphorical terms but of the priest being a vehicle for the personality of Jesus Christ and therefore capable of mirroring Christ's own ministry in the sexuality proper to the Person of Christ as man.

The Vocation of Christ to Man and Woman

The sad series of events which have placed new obstacles in the way of reconciliation between Catholics and Anglicans[74] may well run their course. But it would be a mistake to see this as merely a discussion about words and names (Acts 18:15) which could be as easily dismissed. We are considering the nature of man and woman not from any merely sociological or psychological point of view but from the perspective of the Incarnation. This is written into the creation itself of which Christ is the Lord.

If we so scramble the roles that there is no male and female in our mind we are doing no service to humanity. It will not make us all unisexual, it will just confuse us. As Holloway says "Christ is always going to be for us all the one and unique 'Father' figure, because He is the 'Son' of the Eternal Father, and even in his humanity the most perfect possible expression of the Father. The priest, from the Pope downwards, to the humblest parish priest and assistant, is going to mirror in his personality—which includes his male sexuality—the same relationship to the People of God."[75]

But we also deprive the woman of her unique capacity of showing forth that receptiveness of which the Church and the world has such need. If the man is called to live the headship of Christ as priest, the woman is also called to bring forth the fulness of the gift of one's very being which ultimately is at the heart of our creatureliness. This can be developed if we see the Offertory Procession at Mass as the ministry *to* the altar, of women bringing the fruit of the earth and the work of human hands. Our Lady first brought to God the fruit of the earth and work of her holy womb. The prophetic role of women, so amply demonstrated in the lives of Teresa of Avila and Catherine of Siena, Margaret Clitherow, the Yorkshire housewife and Elizabeth Seton (who after the death of her husband became the foundress of the American Sisters of Charity), stems from an ability to remind the Church of what it must possess: that strength to hear the word of God and heed it. Such was the mark of Mary whom we honour as Mother of the Church, to use the phrase bestowed on her by Pope Paul VI at the end of Vatican II.

Notes

1. March 1977, p.75
2. *Pacem in Terris*, CTS London translation 1963 n.41
3. *Gaudium et Spes* n.60
4. "Teologia de los ministerios" by Bernard Dupuy in *Mysterium Salutis* IV/2, Ediciones Cristiandad, Madrid 1975 p.503
5. *The Second Sex*, Alfred A Knopf, 1952 p.285
6. *Ist Gott ein Mann?* A Röper. Düsseldorf, 1979 p.88
7. "Review and Perspectives on the State of the Development of the Feminine Diaconate" *Diakonia XP* published by the Secretariat of the International Diaconate Centre, Freiburg, Documentation (April 1978) p.27
8. "The Position of Woman as a Problem of Theological Anthropology" in *The Church and Women, A Compendium* (ed. Moll) Ignatius Press, San Francisco, 1988 p.58
9. *The Mary Myth: On the Femininity of God*, Harper and Row, New York 1977, p.147
10. Gilles Quispel, *Gnosis als Weltreligion*, Zurich 1951 p.46
11. To Members of the Study Commission on the Role of Women in Society 18 April 1975, AAS 67 (1975) p.265
12. AAS 62 (1970) p.593
13. "This will place enormous pressure on the Holy Father and it will be all the more difficult for him to uphold the dignity and unique role of women in the Church" Joseph Fessio "Admission of Women to Service at the Altar as Acolytes & Lectors" *The Church & Women* p.184
14. Surah 4:34
15. *Theologia Moralis Compendium*, Marcellinus Zalba, Biblioteca de Autores Cristianos, Madrid 1958 pp.92-93; "far from being timidly submissive" (*Mulieris Dignitatem* n.37) *Casti Conubii* n.27
16. "Whoever as a theologian does not conclusively renounce the category of 'subordination' with all its consequences can be no credible advocate of another answer" Lehman in *The Church & Women* p.24
17. *Mulieris Dignitatem*, n.6
18. Karl Lehman "The Place of Women . . . " in *The Church & Women* pp.27-28
19. *Perelandra* or *Voyage to Venus* ch.16
20. Cf. Louis Bouyer, *Women in the Church*, Ignatius Press, San Francisco 1979 p.130
21. Edward Holloway, *Catholicism, a New Synthesis*, Faith Keyway, Wallington, 1976 p.129
22. *Male and Female* q. Lehman, "The Place of Women . . . " pp.32-33
23. This is developed in Manfred Hauke, *Women in the Priesthood* Ignatius Press, San Francisco 1988 pp.216ff
24. *De Carnis Resurrectione* 6 PL 2, 282
25. *Mulieris Dignitatem* n.2 Cf. *Gaudium et Spes* nn.22.45
26. "Thoughts around the Apostolic Letter 'Dignity of Womanhood' " *Faith* 21,1 (1989) p.6

27. quoted in *Ist Gott ein Mann?* p.79
28. Cf. *What will happen to God?* William Oddie. Ignatius Press 1988
29. *The Tablet* 25 February 1989 p.220
30. *Why Priests?* Hans Küng, Collins/Fontana Glasgow 1972 p.59
31. "Thoughts around the Apostolic Letter 'Dignity of Womanhood' " p.8
32. *Mulieris Dignitatem* n.29
33. Ibid n.30
34. *Casti Conubii* (CTS London translation) n.76
35. Ibid n.75
36. *Mulieris Dignitatem* n.29
37. *Perestroika*, Mikhail Gorbachov. Fontana/Collins Glasgow 1988 p.117
38. 13 June 1987 printed in *The Pope Teaches* CTS London (vol 8) p.236
39. Cf. *The Theology of the Priesthood* Jean Galot. Ignatius Press 1985 p.263
40. *20 Tesis sobre Ser Cristiano*. Ediciones Cristiandad Madrid 1977 p.88
41. *Ministry, A Case for Change*. SCM London 1981 p.97
42. *The Ordination of Women to the Priesthood. A Second Report by The House of Bishops* GS 829 1988 n.37 p.18
43. Text in *Origins* NC News Service 1 July 1976 vol 6 No 6
44. CLSA 24 August 1973
45. "Christian Women in Ecclesiastical Ministry" Agnes Cunningham in *Pro and Con on Ordination of Women* Seabury New York 1977 p.64
46. *La Documentation Catholique* 1633 (1973) p.531
47. March 1977 editorial p.76
48. Cf. G B Gray, *Sacrifice in the Old Testament*. Oxford 1925. pp.184–91; Manfred Hauke, *Women in the Priesthood* p.212
49. Irenaeus *Adversus Haereses* 1.13.2 ML7,579; Tertullian *De Praescriptione Haereticorum* CCL 1 p.221; Augustine *Comm in Epist I Tim 3,1* ML17,470; Letter 75. CSEL 3 pp.817–8; John Chrysostom *De sacerdotio* 3,9 MG48,646
50. Epiphanius, *Adversus Haereses* 78,13 PG 42,736
51. *Constitutiones Apostolicae* III 9.3 in F X Funk Didascalia I p.201
52. Ep 9,26 PL59,55
53. A G Martimort, *Deaconesses*. Ignatius Press, San Francisco 1986 p.156
54. *Dictionaire de Theologie Catholique* I p.21
55. December 11, 1210 q *Decretals* Lib V tit 38, De paenitentia can 10
56. *Inter Insigniores* Ch.1; Cf. also *Code of Canon Law* Canon 1024
57. *The Ordination of Women to the Priesthood. A Second Report* n.162 p.98
58. *Crises Facing the Church*. Paulist Press New York 1975 p.57
59. *Daughters of the Church* Ruth Tucker and Walter Liefeld. Zondervan Grand Rapids 1987 pp.279–81
60. *The Church We Believe In*. Gill and MacMillan. Dublin 1989 p.186
61. *An Open Letter to the Anglican Episcopate*. Grove Books 1988 p.7
62. *Baptism, Eucharist and Ministry*. Faith and Order Paper 111 (1982) p.24. Comprehensiveness in this sense equals *inclusiveness*.
63. III Sent D. 12 A3 Q 1
64. *Summa Theologica* Supplementum Q 39 A1 ad 2.3

65. Cf. *Sexual Order and Holy Order*, Edward Holloway. Faith Keyway Wallington 1975 p.9
66. Text in *Origins*. NC News Service 1 July 1976 Vol 16 No 6
67. March 1977 p.76
68. "Women and the Ministry of Priesthood" G W H Lampe. *Explorations in Theology 8*. SCM London 1981 p.97
69. "Eucharistic Presidency and Women's Ordination" John Austin Baker *Theology* 88 (1985) pp.354-357
70. *Ep. 63,14* CSEL 3,713
71. *Agreed Statement on Ministry and Ordination* n.13
72. *Summa Theologica* III Q 83 A1 ad 3
73. *Mediator Dei* (1947) CTS London Translation n.73. The Vatican II Decree on the Ministry and Life of Priests says "Priests by the anointing of the Holy Spirit are signed with a special character and so are configured to Christ the Priest in such a way that they are able to act in the person of Christ the Head" (n.2)
74. Letter of Pope John Paul to the Archbishop of Canterbury 8 December 1988 (quoted in full in the Appendix). Pope Paul VI had written to Archbishop Donald Coggan on 23 March 1976 about the likelihood of the admission of women to the priesthood in Anglican Churches and stressed the "so grave a new obstacle and threat". q. Commentary on *Inter Insigniores* CTS London 1977 p.28
75. *Sexual Order and Holy Order* p.23

Considerations from the Eastern Churches on Women and the Priesthood

Roman Cholij

Introduction

The Advent of feminist theology in recent times and the demand for women priests occasioned by such theology presents the Christian Church with a new challenge. The church, in its leaders and its theologians, is required to reflect on itself and to examine its reasons for an exclusively male priesthood. The Eastern Churches, composing both the Orthodox Churches and the Eastern Catholic Churches (sometimes referred to as 'uniate' churches for they are in communion with Rome), are in their turn required to make a statement on the question in the light of their own traditions and theology.

Being a relatively new challenge Feminist theology has not yet received an exhaustive examination and study by the Eastern Churches - at least not in all its aspects and implications.[1] Nonetheless, they have made their unequivocal and definitive response to the question of the possibility of a female priesthood: an uncompromising No. This attitude is not to deny - far from it - the special and unique contribution of women to the life of the church, including through diverse official ministries. Nor does it mean that feminist theology is being rejected *in toto*. The church's task is to "test everything; hold fast what is good" (1 Thess 5,21). At the very least the church is receiving a stimulus to help it to sharpen and refine some aspects of its reflective understanding of itself, especially its own 'feminine' characteristics.[2] A lasting positive contribution which may result from today's debate, and which one much desires – especially for the Eastern Churches – is a more developed and more profound understanding of Christ's priesthood.

A First Response

The basic position of the Orthodox Churches regarding the ordination of women to the priesthood is nowhere more concisely and clearly expressed than in the Report of the special meeting of the Anglican-Orthodox Joint Doctrinal Commission, held in Athens in July 1978.[3] After considering the various ministries (diakoniai) which are exercised by women in the church, the report states:

> . . . But, while women exercise this diversity of ministries, it is not possible for them to be admitted to the priesthood. The ordination of women to the priesthood is an innovation, lacking any basis whatever in Holy Tradition. The Orthodox Church takes very seriously the admonition of St. Paul, where the Apostle states with emphasis, repeating himself twice: 'But if we, or an angel from heaven, preaches to you anything else than what we have preached to you, let him be anathema. As we have already said, so I say to you now once more: if anyone preaches to you anything else than what you have received, let him be anathema' (Gal.1.8-9).
> From the time of Christ and the apostles onwards, the Church has ordained only men to the priesthood. Christians today are bound to remain faithful to the example of our Lord, to the testimony of Scripture, and to the constant and

unvarying practice of the Church for two
thousand years. In this constant and unvarying
practice we see revealed the will of God and the
testimony of the Holy Spirit, and we know that
the Holy Spirit does not contradict himself.[4]

The Argument from Sacred Tradition.

The argument from tradition therefore leads the Eastern
churches to reject any possibility of a disciplinary
change in favour of a female priesthood. Some of the
Anglican members of the Athens Commission, who
were in favour of this change, had felt that the church's
tradition must grow and develop if the church is to
remain faithful to its mission to the world. More
particularly they believed that this change was a true
development, and one made under the guidance of the
Holy Spirit. In their view God had called the churches
to produce a major change in the pattern or patterns of
ministry in order to respond to the changes in the
ordering of Society which had occurred.[5]

Implicit in the thinking of these Anglican members of
the commission is an idea of Tradition akin to that
found in secular society - a principle of conservationism,
a way of keeping alive the past, the passing down of
ancient practices and customs (traditions with a small
't'). Tradition would seem to be a somewhat lifeless,
even anachronistic reference to the past and a principle
of inertia, if it stood in the way of necessary change. But
this way of understanding Sacred Tradition (as opposed
to 'mere' traditions with a small 't') is very inadequate,
to say the least.

Tradition, indeed, is the very "critical spirit of the
church",[6] that which *permits* true growth and development rather than being a hinderance to the same. It is
that vital principle which gives the church the means to

distinguish between true movements and manifestations of the Spirit of God and that which comes from false prophets. It is the very embodiment of the life and thought of the Church which, in the Spirit, is the life and thought of Christ (cf. Phil 2, 1-2). For the Church is Christ's mystical body – alive, pulsating and vibrant with the Holy Spirit.

Tradition provides the internal continuity for the church that Christ had willed, no matter in what age or circumstance or condition it finds itself. It provides today's church with its vital and real link with the church of the New Testament. It is like the 'soul' that unites a person in his old age to his infancy. Sacred Tradition is not static but living and creative:

> "It is important . . . to distinguish between innovations and the creative continuity of Tradition. We Orthodox see the ordination of women, not as part of this creative continuity, but as a violation of the apostolic faith and the order of the Church".[7]

The creativity of Tradition lies in the fact that it makes Christian truth, based on the revelation of God as written in the Scriptures, *ever present*. It lies in the fact that the members of the church are, through Tradition, given the mind of Christ and given the capacity to be able to respond, as Christ would respond, to the needs of the contemporary world. Tradition, in its creative continuity, *is* already the action of the Holy Spirit; "it belongs to the Holy Spirit which dwells in the church",[8] even constituting the "entire life of the Church in the Holy Spirit".[9] There can therefore be no clash between Tradition and the work of the Holy Spirit in today's church, for this would be a contradiction in terms: "Every Kingdom divided against itself is laid waste, and no city or house divided against itself will stand" (Mt. 12, 25).

Tradition is related in a similar way to Scripture; they are correlative and do not stand against each other as separate sources of revelation. The Moscow Agreed Statement of 1976 reads:

> Any disjunction between Scripture and Tradition such as would treat them as two separate 'sources of revelation' must be rejected. The two are correlative. We affirm (i) that Scripture is the main criterion whereby the Church tests traditions to determine whether they are truly part of Holy Tradition or not; (ii) that Holy Tradition completes Holy Scripture in the sense that it safeguards the integrity of the biblical message.[10]

Scripture, therefore, 'lives' in Tradition: "We know, receive, and interpret Scripture through the Church and in the Church."[11]

Since Tradition 'makes present' the eternal truths of the Gospel, there are many ways or modes in which Sacred Tradition is expressed. Dogmatic tradition – the 'rule of faith' – especially as found in the Ecumenical Councils – is of supreme importance, but does not exhaust the modes of expression of Sacred Tradition. The lives of the saints have an important role, and the tested means of fostering the spiritual life are likewise expressions of the church's inner life and its Sacred Tradition. The liturgical worship of the church is of central importance, and, for the East, provides the most direct and easily grasped reason against a female priesthood. Canonical tradition is also an aspect and mirror of Sacred Tradition, in so far as it expresses the unchangeable truth of divine revelation. Many individual disciplines are reformable and do not in themselves reflect Tradition. The discipline concerning the maleness of the Priest is, however, a part of divine revelation and is as a result irreformable.

Some Theological Presuppositions

Having established that Tradition is more than a perception of the church's past, more than a form of 'conservationism', one naturally wishes to seek a greater understanding of the theological reasons for exclusion of women priests within the creative-continous Tradition of the church, which presents to us the Faith. Faith seeking understanding is, after all, a good working (Anselmian) definition for theology. The most complete approach to date from the Orthodox Churches (as opposed to the works of individual authors) to develop this theology is to be found in the conclusions of the inter-Orthodox consultation: "On the place of the Woman in the Orthodox Church and the question of the Ordination of Women", held in Rhodes, Greece, 30 Oct-7 Nov 1988. [12] In this document the question of the male character of the priesthood is firmly set within a more general context of theology: within Christology, Pneumatology, Ecclesiology, Sacramental and Liturgical Theology. It is made clear, therefore, that the particular subject of the male priesthood cannot be isolated from the rest of fundamental theology, for all form parts of one vital whole. Conversely, the postulate of a female priesthood comes from a broader-based feminist theology which challenges many other aspects of traditional Christian teaching. [13] Many individual areas of theology would need a thorough exposition before one could give expression to a totally adequate investigation of the male priesthood. For our purposes it is sufficient to underline certain basic ideas on the nature of the church and the nature of the priesthood before proceeding further.

a) *The Church as Mystery*

If the church were to be regarded solely as an external institution without an inseparable and intrinsic unity with its 'charismatic' aspect, then any hierarchical system, especially if predominantly male, would appear to some to be an intolerable male clericalism. In such a church, ministries would be understood as deputable offices, and democratization – in keeping with modern secular mentality – would seem to demand an equal share of such offices by women.

The church, nonetheless, is not just a sociological entity, comprised of members and leaders. It is above all a *mystery* which "cannot be defined or fully described".[14] It is the mystery of the inauguration of the Kingdom of God in this world: the mystery of the incarnate Son of God still present in the world, who pours out His Spirit on his people to transform them 'into his likeness'(2 Cor 3.18). Through the sign and instrumentality of the sacraments – the 'holy mysteries' – Christ's saving grace is made available to his people, making them "partakers of the divine nature"(2 Pet 1.4). Because the church is sacramental it is also hierarchical. Leadership is for service, and the sacramental ministry exists in order to serve the sacramentality of the church, making it an effective sign of salvation to the world. The church, therefore, does not 'belong' to its members, the People of God, but to Christ, the Head (Eph.3.17). It is something greater than the sum of all its constitutive members, for it is fundamentally a supernatural reality, and it is because of this supernatural, mysterious character that no number of doctrinal formulae can exhaustively express its reality. Thus the language of communication needs the service of the symbol, figure, image and type. Christ proclaimed the mystery of the Kingdom in imagery, as did the ministers of the Apostolic Church: Head-Body,

Bridgroom–Bride (Eph 1.22; Col 1.18; 1 Cor 12.27; Eph 5.27; 2 Cor 11.2). Such symbolism communicates truths to the heart as well as to the head. This language, as much as the language of dogmatic definition, is *normative* for the church, for in it the church seeks an ever greater understanding of itself. Because these symbols express the supernatural (and thus supra-rational) character of the church, they cannot be arbitrarily exchanged or substituted, no matter what the rational argumentation for such a change might be. The symbolic meaning of 'father' cannot have an equivalent in the word 'mother'; therefore we cannot pray 'Our Mother' in place of 'Our Father' without doing violence to our relationship with God. To reverse the roles of Bride and Bridegroom, Spouse and Husband in relation to the church and Christ, would do violence to the church's understanding of itself. It would undermine and ultimately destroy the Christian revelation. A distortion of the different symbolic roles of the male and female sex, especially with regard to the male priest, who is a symbol and image of Christ as Bridegroom, would lead to a distortion of man's "understanding of the redemption of the deepest aspects of his humanity".[15]

b) *The Sacramental Priesthood is Christ's*

Christ alone, the Head of the Church, is forever the only Mediator and great High Priest, reconciling humanity to God through His whole work of salvation and His sacrifice on Golgotha (2 Cor 5:18-20; Heb 2:17;3.1). He, therefore, is in the profoundest sense the sole celebrant of all the sacraments. He it is who baptises, who offers the Eucharistic sacrifice, who reconciles sinners in the sacrament of penance. All the faithful, by virtue of their baptismal 'royal' priesthood

(1 Pet 2.9) are called to bear the image of Christ, to witness to Him in their daily lives, and offer daily spiritual sacrifices through Him to the Father. The 'sacrificial' royal priesthood, nonetheless, can exist only in relation to the ministerial, "sacerdotal" or "special" priesthood[16] whereby Christ's Eucharistic sacrifice is made present as it was on Golgotha. Unlike the royal priesthood, only a few are called to this special ministry whereby Christ is made present 'iconically' as Head of his Body. This special gift "is granted to the Church through the grace of the Holy Spirit at the sacrament of ordination (cheirotonia) by which those being ordained are made "servants of Christ and stewards of the mysteries of God" (l Cor 4.1). "It was given by the Lord to the Apostles and their successors in the apostolic ministry of *episkope* for the people of God".[17] This gift is 'given by the Lord', 'granted to the Church'. It is not an 'elected' office where somebody who 'feels' the rightness and appropriateness of this task seeks deputation from the People of God to represent them before God. Before being an individual calling, priestly ordination is a gift to the whole church. It is first and foremost *Christ's* gift and *His* election, since the Eucharistic sacrifice and priestly mediatorship is *His* sacrifice and *His* mediatorship. In the Divine Liturgy of St. John Chrysostom the priest prays the following, just before the liturgy of the Offering: " . . . and by the power of your Holy Spirit strengthen us whom You have appointed to this your ministry . . . . " At the liturgy of the Offering he says: " . . . for to minister unto You is great and awesome even for the very powers of heaven . . . You became our High Priest, and as Master of all conferred upon us the priestly function of this Liturgy and unbloody sacrifice. For You are the One who offer and are offered . . . . " During the Divine Liturgy of Saint Basil the Great, just before the Epiclesis, the priest prays: "Therefore, Most Holy Lord, we also sinners and

Your unworthy servants called by You to serve at Your
holy altar, not by reason of righteousness . . . but by
reason of your love and mercy . . . ."

*Foundational Theological Arguments for the Maleness of the
Priesthood*

Whom does the Lord call to give the sacramental grace
of the priesthood? Clearly, the church has to discern
Christ's will from the example of his attitude and the
practice of the apostles. This is the foundational
argument for the maleness of the Priesthood in the
Western Catholic Church as in the Eastern Churches.[18]
The 1988 Inter-Orthodox consultation document expresses its position thus:

> ' . . . the impossibility of the ordination of
> women to the special priesthood as founded in
> the tradition of the Church has been expressed in
> these ecclesiastically rooted positions:
> (a) On the example of our Lord Jesus Christ,
> who did not select any woman as one of His
> Apostles;
> (b) on the example of the Theotokos, who did
> not exercise the sacramental priestly function in
> the Church, even though she was made worthy
> to become the mother of the Incarnate Son and
> Word of God;
> (c) on the criterion of analogy, according to
> which, if the exercise of episcope by women
> were permitted, then it should have been exer-
> cised by the Theotokos.
> (d) on the Apostolic Tradition, according to
> which the Apostles, following the example of the
> Lord, never ordained any women to this special
> Priesthood of episcope in the Church;

(e) on some Pauline teachings concerning the position of women in the Church.[19]

Each one of these points warrants a full discussion, especially in light of the counter-arguments offered by those who promote the idea of a female priesthood. However, such a discussion would be outside the particular scope of this presentation. The reader, instead, is well-advised to consult the masterly work of Manfred Hauke, *Women in the Priesthood* (Ignatius Press 1986) for such a study.[20]

The Gospels, the writings of the Apostle Paul and the life and example of the New Testament Church were the norm or rule of faith and discipline for the church of the subsequent post-apostolic and patristic ages. To the witness of these ages we now turn.

The Witness of the Early Church and the Fathers

Already in the early church there were sectarian groups who permitted a female priesthood and who allowed women to take upon themselves other ministerial functions related to ministerial leadership, such as public preaching and baptising. That this was contrary to the rule of faith is seen in the writings of certain of the early church fathers and in some of the oldest ecclesiastical documents that have been preserved: the Didascalia, the Apostolic Constitutions and the Apostolic Church Order. To understand why the female priesthood was promoted among certain sections of the ancient Christian church, some acquaintance with the system of thought that prevailed in these communities is needed.[21]

In the second century AD the church had to struggle with the heresy of *Gnosticism* - a complicated belief system which was to return in one form after another in the centuries that followed. Characteristic of the heterodox Gnostic belief system was its hostility towards the body and all things material, for these it deemed to belong to the 'darkened' level of being from which man had to free himself in order to enter into the 'divine' world of light. Furthermore, the difference between the sexes was regarded as a limitation to be overcome, for the 'primal' human being was judged to be 'androgynous' (male-female) made in the likeness of an androgynous (male-female) God.[22] Other aspects of Gnosticism include the doctrine that God and Man have essentially the same origin: God being immanent in creation and having no transcendence. The ultimate implication of these heretical beliefs is that a religion is created in which God is fashioned in the image and likeness of man.[23]

If, according to the tenets of Gnosticism, sexual differentiation is not part of the *true* order of creation, nor part of the order of redemption – where through grace differentiation is overcome – then women should 'naturally' be free to take on all the activities of men in the church community. This included public preaching and offering the Eucharistic sacrifice. Christian liberation implied liberation from all the distinctions derived from 'bodiliness'.[24]

Apocryphal writings suffused with these ideas flourished. The apocryphal Gospel of Thomas, for example, has Christ saying these words:

'If you . . . make the masculine and the feminine into but one thing, so that the masculine is not masculine and the feminine is not feminine . . . then you will enter the kingdom.'

'Behold I will educate her (Mary) in such a way as to make her masculine, so that she will also become a living spirit equal to you men. For a woman who makes herself a man will enter the kingdom of heaven.'[25]

As a result of this type of anthropology there was a blurring not only of the distinctions between male and female ministries, but also between laity and clergy. Such obfuscation is far from rare in modern writings too.

In the second century Ireneus, Bishop of Lyons (but hailing from the East), condemned the teaching of the Gnostics as found in Asia Minor. He mentions the abusive practice of women celebrating the Eucharist who felt impelled to do so by the Holy Spirit.[26]

Disciplinary abuses sanctioned by the appeal to 'direct guidance by the Holy Spirit' were common amongst Montanists. Montanism was another heresy of the early church which brought down the wrath of many an 'anti-charismatic' church father. By the 4th century the rule against ordination of women was also being broken. Not uncommon, in justification of this practice, was the appeal to the words of St. Paul to the Galatians - 3:28:

'There is neither Jew nor Greek, there is neither slave nor freeman, there is neither male nor female; for you are all one in Christ Jesus.'

Epiphanius, Bishop of Salamis (died 403 AD) replies to the Montanists, using counter-arguments from Holy Scripture, and especially from St. Paul. He would not deny that the saving work of grace is directed to all, without any distinctions of race or condition, but the authority invested in the priesthood, both from the voice of creation and from the redemption, can only be given to men.[27] More about this church father later.

Montanism had not been immune to the subtle influences of the pagan socio-cultural milieu in which it had originated, especially that form which permitted priestesses. Phrygia, in Asia Minor, had known a particularly strong cult to the godmother Cybele. Montanus, who founded the sect there, may even have been, in his pre-Christian days, a priest of Cybele. An androgynous Christ would have been for the former followers of Cybele a happy substitute for their dethroned goddess. 'In the form of a woman . . . Christ came to me in radiant garb . . . ' was reportedly the claim of the visioness Priscilla.[28]

Origen (died circa 253 AD) joins the dispute against those Montanists who, following the example of Priscilla, engaged in a public-official teaching. [29] This is an indirect statement against priestesses, since public teaching was exclusive to those invested with the office of the 'episcope'. Tertullian (died circa 225 AD), writing against Gnostics of the same tendency, makes this most clear: 'It is forbidden for a woman . . . to teach, to baptize to sacrifice or to presume to the rank of male office, not to mention priestly service.'[30]

Hippolytus of Rome tells the same story, this time in regard to widows entering into the 'order' of widows. The second century 'Apostolic Tradition' states:

'When a widow is accepted into the widowhood, then she is not ordained, but appointed as such . . . . One should not lay hands upon her, for she does not offer up the sacrifice and performs no liturgical service. Ordination (cheirotonia) takes place, namely, for the clergy with a view to liturgical service.'[31]

A fourth century version of this text, originating in Egypt, makes plain that widows do not have the essential pre-condition of maleness for ordination. For widows too 'the prescriptions of the apostle are valid. They are not allowed to be ordained, but rather, one should pray over them; for ordination is for men'.[32]

Any possible subversion of the natural order of things is a delusion of the devil. So wrote Firmilian, a bishop of Caesarea, to Cyprian of Carthage (died circa 258 AD) when discussing a possessed woman (possibly a Montanist Priestess):

'Through the deceptions and illusions of the demon, this woman had previously set about deluding believers in a variety of ways. Among the means by which she had deluded many was daring to pretend that, through proper invocation, she consecrated bread and performed the Eucharist. She offered up the Sacrifice to the Lord in a liturgical act that corresponded to the usual rites.'[33]

The Didascalia and the office of Deaconess

The *Didascalia* is an interesting work from the third century, which probably originated East of the region of Antioch. Among other things, it regulates the various tasks of women in the Christian community, but it also introduces – probably for the first time – the female office of deaconess.[34] Although the deaconess had an official position in the church, as with other women no official public preaching was permitted to her: 'It is not in order to teach that you women . . . are appointed, but in order to pray and to petition the Lord.'[35] The deaconess also had an exact role to fulfil. In a 'patriarchal' society which insisted on strict separation of the sexes she was to visit the sick and to minister generally to women in their female living quarters. Her more important function, however, was to help at the baptism of women. She would continue with the pre-baptismal anointing of the body of a female after the male minister initiated the process. She would instruct the newly baptized women on a regular basis.[36] Presupposed, therefore, was a sound and adequate knowledge of church doctrine. The ban on public preaching, consequently, could not have been due to 'impropriety' or to lack of education (as might have been the case with the laity and widows). The decisive argument for the Didiscalia is the behaviour and attitude of Jesus:

'For it is not to teach that you women . . . are anointed . . . . . For he, God the Lord, Jesus Christ our Teacher, sent us, the Twelve, out to teach the (chosen) people and the pagans. But there were female disciples among us: Mary of Magdala, Mary the daughter of

Jacob and the other Mary; he did not, however, send them out with us to teach the people. For, had it been necessary that women should teach, then our Teacher would have directed them to instruct along with us.'[37]

The Apostolic Constitutions

The *Apostolic Constitutions* is a document from the fourth century AD (circa 380) also probably originating from around Antioch. Here, as in some of the previous authorities cited, the ban on public teaching is expressly connected with the prohibition of ordination to the priesthood:

'If, in the foregoing, we do not allow women to teach, how can anyone agree that they – in contempt of their nature – should assume the office of priest? For it is ignorant heathen ungodliness that leads to the ordination of priestesses for female deities, but not the command of Christ'.[38]

The 'command of Christ' is therefore normative for the church, and it is, over and above other reasons of appropriateness, the basis of the *regula fidei*. From the *Constitutions* we also learn more about the function of deaconesses; they are to exchange the kiss of peace with the women in the eucharisitic assembly, and are particularly responsible for the female part of the congregation – acting as doorkeepers for them. No women could presume to speak to the higher clergy without having first spoken to the deaconess.[39] Included also is a prayer for the consecration of deaconesses. It follows that for deacons, but the content is quite different. The function of the two ministries are clearly distinguished:

'A deaconess does not bless, and performs none of the duties carried out by a priest or deacon . . . '.[40]

The exclusion of the deaconess, or of any other

woman, from 'sacerdotal' service, cannot be explained by assuming that the church authorities had a low regard for women. It was not because of any *inferiority*, but because of the consciousness of Christ's *command* left to the church as the *regula fidei*. Deaconesses, in particular, although set apart from the priestly hierarchy, had a recognised ecclesiastical dignity and were considered, for example by Epiphanius, as constituting part of the clergy.[41] Many of the deaconesses from this period of the church's history contributed greatly to the life of the church, and this fact is recorded by the numerous deaconess saints who feature in the Byzantine Liturgical Calendar. Examples are St. Macrina (July 19th), the sister and teacher of St. Basil and Gregory of Nyssa; St. Nonna (August 6th), wife of Gregory of Nazianus the elder; St. Melonia (December 31st), St. Theosibia (Jan 10th), wife of Gregory of Nyssa (she was ordained a deaconess after her husband became a bishop) and St. Olympia (July 25th), close friend of St. John Chrysostom.

Apostolic Church Order

The last of the documents to consider is that fragmentary testimony to the fourth century Egyptian Church known as the *Apostolic Church Order*. A literary device, a conversation between the twelve apostles, is used to transmit the doctrine of the church. One of the discussions concerns the question of priesthood for women:

'Andrew says, 'Brothers, it would be useful to institute an office for women.' Peter says, 'We have already made preparations for that. But regarding the sacrifice of the Body and Blood, we need to express ourselves more precisely.'

John says, 'You have forgotten something, brothers:

When our Master asked for the bread and the cup and blessed them with the words: "This is my body and my blood", he did not allow the women to join us' [for the consecration].

Martha says 'That was only because of Mary, since he saw her smiling.' Mary says, 'That was not because I had laughed. For, before then he had said to us, as he taught, that the weak will be saved by the strong' [that is man by woman].

Cephas says, 'Undoubtedly you will recall that it is not appropriate for women to pray while standing, but rather, while sitting on the ground.'[42]

In this interesting document the place of women in the ministries of the church is assured: 'We have already made preparations . . .' says Peter, the Prince of the Apostles. Indeed, elsewhere in this same document the institution of widows is established, who are to devote themselves to prayer and to community care. The special ministry of the priesthood, nonetheless, is emphatically denied to women. This is done by recalling both the actions of the Master and his (apocryphal) words. One notes that it is Mary, the one given to the contemplation of revealed truth, and not her 'activist' sister Martha, who was not possessed of the same gift of spiritual insight, who was able to recall the Master's words. Understanding is the fruit of contemplation. The point established by the conversation, and by the author of this work, is that it is by the *will of Christ* that women are excluded from 'praying while standing', that is from offering the eucharistic sacrifice.

Epiphanius

The fullest statement on this subject from any church father of the period being considered, comes from

Bishop Epiphanius of Salamis (Constantia), a great defender of church tradition. Reference has already been made to this bishop's stance against the Montanists. However, he also had cause to take up his pen against certain Collyridian women, who had transferred the pagan cult of a goddess to Mary. These heretics also had priestesses:

'It is reported that certain women there in Arabia (that is in the region east of Palestine) have introduced this absurd teaching from Thracia: how they offer up a sacrifice of bread rolls in the name of the Ever Virginal (that is, of Mary) and hold their meetings in that very name, and how they undertake something that far exceeds proper measure in the name of the Holy Virgin. In an unlawful and blasphemous ceremony, they ordain women, through whom they offer up the sacrifice in the name of Mary. This means that the entire proceeding is godless and sacrilegious, a perversion of the message of the Holy Spirit; in fact, the whole thing is diabolical and a teaching of the impure spirit.'[43]

Epiphanius' answer to the practice of women priests was to consider sacred history and then to conclude: 'Nowhere did a woman serve as a priestess.'[44] He was certainly aware of the practice of pagan religions, but this, by the will of God, was not to be the case in the true religion. It was not because of inferiority that women are excluded from the priesthood, for the Blessed Virgin, greatest of all God's creatures, would have been the first to have been chosen:

'If women were to be charged by God with entering the priesthood or with assuming ecclesiastical office then in the New Covenant it would have devolved upon no one more than Mary to fulfil a priestly function. She was invested with so great an honour as to be allowed to provide a dwelling in her womb for the heavenly God and King of all things, the Son of God . . . . . But he did not find this [the conferring of priesthood] good. Not even baptizing was entrusted to her; otherwise, Christ could better have been baptized by her than by John'.[45]

Some of the remarks Epiphanius makes in his vigorous rebuttal of the errors of the Collyridians would make a modern woman smart:

'For the female sex is easily misled, weak and without much sense.'

'May we therefore be on our guard, servants of God! Let us array ourselves in the sensibleness of men, so that we dispel this madness of women.'[46]

However, before accusing Epiphanius of simply being a misogynist one has to remember that he was writing – in the true polemical style of his age – in order to confute not to instruct. Ridicule was considered a proper tool to put right the foolishness of women involved in this 'diabolical' heresy. His manner of debate and his occasional unguarded expressions should not obscure the fact that he could also express his highest regard for the female sex, as instanced by his respectful consideration of deaconesses and his devotion to Mary the Mother of God. What was at stake for him was not the qualities of women, but the will of Christ and the apostolic tradition:

'From this bishop (the brother of the Lord, James in Jerusalem) and the just-named apostles, the successions of bishops and presbyters in the house of God has been established. Never was a women called to these . . . . . According to the evidence of Scripture, there were, to be sure, the four daughters of the evangelist Philip, who engaged in prophecy, but they were not priestesses.'[47]

Epiphanius' testimony was passed on to others by two other great lights of the Christian church: Augustine, in the West and John Damascene, in the East (the last of the Greek Fathers).[48] St. John Chrysostom, a contemporary of Epiphanius, considers the calling of Peter as being the exemplar for priestly vocations. In his treatise 'On the Priesthood', he writes:

'For the tasks that I just listed could readily be performed by many of the subordinates, too, not only men, but women as well. If, however, it is a matter of being entrusted with direction of a church and with the care of so many souls, then, first of all, the entire female sex must step back from so great a task, but also the majority of males.'[49]

Elsewhere in his writings John Chrysostom confirms the ban on public teaching: this did not exclude the possibility of a non-official teaching position.[50] Among his associates and acquaintances were women who had a very good theological formation. In the secular realm there were also capable women rulers. But it was the will of Christ and the authority of St. Paul that made it clear to this great eastern father that women could not become priests.

This is the same motif which underlies all the forms of testimony of the early church which we have considered. All are expressions of Sacred Tradition, *the* Tradition, unvarying and constant on this fundamental issue. Another aspect of Tradition must now be considered, which will form the concluding section of this essay: the liturgical life of the church and the iconic significance of the priest in liturgy.

The Priest as Liturgical Icon of Christ.
The very 'heart' of Sacred Tradition is liturgical worship, for in it 'is the revelation and realization by the church of her own real nature'[51]. Dogma and worship are thus inseparable:

'Faith and worship are inseparable. Dogmas are not abstract ideas existing in and for themselves, but revealed and saving truths and realities intended to bring mankind into communion with God. Through the liturgical life of the church creation comes to share in this saving reality . . . The great affirmations of Christian doctrine have their liturgical formulation and expression; all the saving truths of the faith are doxologically and liturgically appropriated.'[52].

1. *The Nature of the Icon*.

One of the ways in which Christian truths have been liturgically 'appropriated' – especially in the Byzantine East – is through the Icon. 'Icon' (eikon) means 'image'. Iconography is a *Liturgical* art which 'images' or represents the saving teaching of the church, through its reference to some concrete event or person in sacred history, or through its referal to an example of the state of transfiguration and glorification found in the saints. Its purpose is not to give aesthetic pleasure or to fill out architectural space; it is to make present, through the medium of the image, the Gospel. 'What the word transmits through the ear', says St. Basil the Great, 'that painting silently shows through the image'.[53] The Icon is therefore a vehicle of the Gospel, a means of transmitting Sacred Tradition and making it present liturgically. An Icon becomes a *part* of liturgical worship because, unlike much of religious art, it is *venerated*. Of course, this religious response is directed towards the prototype of the image: 'the honour shown to the Icon passes to the prototype'[54]. Thus for the Byzantine worshipper, icons do not just 'serve' the Christian religion: they are part of it.[55]

The composition of icons, how an image is painted, must as a consequence be controlled by theological criteria – in the same way as preaching or sacred music must be – for the iconographer acts as a transmitter of the faith. His first rule is the rule of the Gospel. The fathers of the Seventh Ecumenical Council (Nicaea II), held in 787, stated that:

'We preserve, without innovations, all the church traditions established for us, whether written or unwritten, one of which is icon-painting as corresponding to what the gospels preach and relate . . . For if one is shown by the other, the one is incontestably made clear by the other.'[56].

Commenting on this council one theologian writes:

'Thus the icon is placed on a level with the Holy Scriptures and with the cross, as one of the forms of revelation and knowledge of God, in which divine and human will and action become blended. Apart from its direct meaning, each alike is a reflection of the higher world; each alike is a symbol of spirit contained in them. Consequently, the meaning of both the word and the image, their role and significance, are the same.'[57].

In eastern church history the icon has played an important role in combating heresies and in upholding and promoting true doctrine. Against the Arian heresy, the signs Alpha and Omega were painted by the figure of Christ, to stress His Divinity, which was denied by the heretics. After Ephesus, the triumphal image of the Theotokos was painted with the Divine Child enthroned in glory. At the time of the Seventh Ecumenical Council, which condemned the iconoclasts, the icon defended the very truth of the incarnation. Thus the icon became the liturgical conserver of christological and trinitarian dogma. But even more than its pedagogic function – or rather together with it – the icon is a means of *entering into contact* with the person or the event represented, and thus it becomes a means of grace. It is a means of experiencing the communion of saints, where the past, present and future of the Divine Kingdom, the celestial and the worldly are made one. 'The more frequently they (that is icons) are seen', says Nicaea II 'the more those who behold them are aroused to remember and desire the prototypes and to give them greeting and the veneration of honour; not indeed true worship, which according to our faith, is due to God alone.'[58].

The relevance of iconic theology to the theme of the male priesthood is found in the fact that in eastern thought, the priest is considered to be the 'liturgical icon' of Christ. A woman lay theologian of the Orthodox church writes:

'In offering the unbloody sacrifice . . . the bishop (or the priest) becomes . . . the icon of the word incarnate. It is this iconic character of the figure of the priest in Orthodox worship that, it seems to me, embodies the strongest argument against the admission of women to the sacramental priesthood.'[59].

In order to understand this argument of iconic representation a number of considerations have to be made concerning the very possibility of an iconic representation of Christ.

2. Icon of Christ.

The very reason for iconographic art in spiritual worship is the reality of the Incarnation and, through it, the transfiguration of all of material creation. St. John Damascene expresses this most aptly:

'In times past, God, without body and form could in no way be represented. But now since God has appeared in flesh and lived among men, I can depict that which is visible of God. I do not venerate matter, but I venerate the Creator of matter, who became matter for me, who condescended to live in matter, and also through matter accomplished my salvation; and I do not cease to respect the matter through which my salvation is accomplished.'[60].

Iconic representation of Christ thus expresses a profound christological truth, namely, that the second person of the Blessed Trinity, the Logos, without ceasing in his divinity to be invisible, uncircumscribable, and unrepresentable, has truly assumed into the unity of his one person, a complete, individual and concrete human nature which is visible, circumscribable and representable. Put the other way round, it is this understanding of the Incarnation that makes orthodox iconic representation of Christ possible. Iconoclasm – the heresy that denies any true depictability of Christ – attacks the very basis of Christianity. It was at the height of iconoclasm that the universal church – when East and West were still united – gathered in its Seventh Ecumenical Council (Nicaea II) on October 23rd 787 AD to vindicate the use and veneration of icons of Christ. By so doing, it also re-affirmed and defended the christological doctrines of previous ecumenical councils, especially the two following Chalcedon. Constantinople II (553 AD) had developed the doctrine of the two natures in one person or 'hypostasis' of Christ, which had been originally defined at Chalcedon (451 AD). It did this by clarifying that the one hypostasis is the Second Person of the Blessed Trinity, the pre-existent divine hypostasis of the Word. There could be no confusion of the hypostatic order with the essential or with nature.[61].

The argument of the iconoclasts was that Christ could not be depicted since what would be portrayed would be just his human nature (which was indeed visible and circumscribable), but not his divine nature (which is invisible and uncircumscribable). The Christ portrayed would not, therefore, be the Christ of the Gospels, the incarnate Son of God. Depicting Christ in this way would be to preach a Christ with confused natures (Monophysitism) or with only a human nature (Nestorianism). The iconoclasts claimed, furthermore, that the Word assumed into his divine person not a human *person* (creating a trinity of four persons), but a human *nature*. Christ's human nature is universal. He is *universal* man, not a particular man; he cannot therefore be depicted in the artist's colours. Such was the iconoclast position.

The response of the defenders of iconic representability (the iconodules) was to point out that there was an essential error in the premises of the iconoclast argument. There was a root misunderstanding of the hypostatic union. St Theodore Studite (759-826 AD), a great defender of the theology of Nicaea II, pointed out that:

'It is the hypostasis of the incarnate word and not his essence which is represented in the icons of Christ.'[62].

Furthermore, common human nature, which Christ assumed into his divine hypostasis, only subsists in *individuals*. The Word assumed not an abstract idea of manhood, but a complete and concrete human nature. Thus the divine hypostasis of the Word truly becomes *this* man, Jesus Christ of Nazareth.

'Iconoclasm's notion of an indeterminate humanity is a subtle Docetism. Universals are apprehended by the intellect; individuals are seen with the eyes. Were Christ's nature universal and not individual, He could only be 'touched' by mind and thought, and his humanity would be an illusion.'[63].

The hypostatic union, in fact, guarantees both the individualism and the inclusiveness of Christ as man. Christ's human nature is not, according to the theology of St. Theodore, hypostatized in an hypostasis of its own, nor is it wholly without an hypostasis; it is 'enhypostatized' in the divine hypostasis of the Word. Thus Christ's humanity is supremely personal – but it is personalised in a divine person.[64] Iconic depiction would not create a 'fourth' person of the Blessed Trinity, nor does it give rise to a Nestorian or Monophysite Christ, since icons do not portray natures as such.

3. Icon of Christ in relation to modern theological tendencies.
Those who claim that Christ's maleness was but a peripheral and not a necessary attribute of his humanity, fail to consider that his hypostatic union was a

hypostasis of a concrete *individual* human being. Otherwise Christ, in his humanity, would be a 'ghost' and as such would not have accomplished the redemption by his real life and his real death on the cross. The resurrectional 'shedding' of Christ's male bodiliness – as taught by modern 'resurrectional spiritualists' was condemned by the fathers of Nicaea II as an Iconoclast Paschal Monophysitism.[65]. The reality of the hypostatic union means that even after the resurrection Christ retained those qualities which were constitutive of his concrete individual human nature.

Finally, the feminine thesis of the 'androgynous' Christ, namely Christ being in his human nature a male-female, represents a christological error, a misunderstanding of Christ's incarnation. It is the same error of intellectualism, found first in Gnosticism and later among the iconoclasts.

4. *The Priest as Icon of Christ.*

The preceding considerations make apparent the impossibility of a female iconic representation of Christ the priest. Affirmations to the contrary are really a modern variant of iconoclasm, a denial of the individualised humanity assumed into Christ's hypostasis. The icon of Christ makes present the *hypostasis* of Christ not his human *nature* which he shares with all men and women. But for an image to represent its prototype there must be a resemblance sensible to the eyes. The resemblance is precisely in the concrete individual *male* form of the enhypostatised human nature of Christ. A female representation would be a representation of a *ghostly* Christ. In other words, the denial of the necessary male resemblance in an icon of Christ, is the denial of the depictability of Christ. This is the iconoclast heresy. A female priesthood would, and as far as it currently exists does, usher in a new docetism in the Christian religion.

It was none other than that giant among iconodule

theologians, St. Theodore Studite, who gives us the clearest formula of the priest's iconic relationship to Christ. In his *Seven Chapters against the Iconoclasts*, he explains why a priest blesses with the sign of the cross, rather than with an icon of Christ:

'Standing before God and men, the priest in his priestly invocations is the representation of Christ. For the Apostle says, "There is one God and one mediator between God and men, the man Christ Jesus" (1 Timothy 2,5). Thus the priest is an icon of Christ.'[66].

The understanding of the priest being an 'image' or 'representation' of Christ has been long established in Tradition, beginning with the Apostle Paul:

'We come therefore as Christ's ambassadors; it is as if God were appealing to you through us.' (2 Corinthians 5,20), and:

'You welcome me as an angel of God, even as Christ Jesus' (Galatians 4,14).

St Ignatius of Antioch (died circa 107) says:

'The bishop presides as the image of God'[67].

Dionysius the Pseudo-Areopagite (6th Century), states that the bishop brings:

' . . . Jesus Christ before our eyes . . . ' and thus 'shows in sensible fashion and in image that which is the very life of our soul: he reveals how Christ himself came out of his mysterious, divine sanctuary out of love for man and took on human form, becoming totally incarnate, but without confusion . . . ' [68].

St Germanus of Constantinople (died 733) describes how:

'The ascent of the bishop to the throne and his blessing the people signifies that the Son of God, having completed the economy of salvation, raised his hands, and blessed his holy disciples . . . .'[69].

Similar examples could be multiplied. These ideas, of the priest being the image or icon of Christ, are connected in a more general way with the patristic tradition concerning ordination.

In this tradition the priest, through ordination by the bishop, receives Christ's indelible seal or mark[70] This paved the way for the later scholastic doctrine of the priest being a 'sign of Christ the Mediator.' the 'bearer of the image of Christ'[71].

Implications of the iconic theology of the priesthood.

The iconic theology of the priesthood, which we have been considering, leads to the conclusion that the maleness of the priest is postulated not only by traditional sacramental theology, but by the reality of the incarnation itself. If the priest is considered to be the image or *icon* of Christ, it is because in his mediatorial role – his 'priestly invocations' – , in his role of offering the eucharistic sacrifice and of forgiving sins, he makes Christ really (though mysteriously) present as Head of the Church, as High Priest, as Master and Lord. Iconic theology stresses the distinctiveness of the image and its prototype; there is no fusion of essence, but a real identity of hypostasis or person. This identity occurs as a result of Christ's sacramental seal in a baptized male subject. Hence, though there are many ordained priests, there is only one High Priest, though there are many mediators, there is only one Mediator between God and man – Jesus Christ. The priest's iconic relationship to Christ, furthermore, rightly makes him an object of veneration, the veneration of *honour* due to all icons.

This is because the honour paid to an icon always passes on to the prototype, and 'he who reveres the image reveres in it the hypostasis represented'.[72] Since the priest makes Christ present liturgically, the honour paid to a priest *qua* priest, is honour paid to Christ.

The custom of kissing the hand of a priest or bishop (still very much practised in countries of the East) is justified in the same way as the kissing of an icon of

Christ, or the kissing of the Book of Gospels, which can be considered the *verbal* icon of Christ. In all cases the icon is a *relational* entity, so that even if the image is blurred – a tatty Gospel, a poorly painted icon, an unworthy priest – the act of veneration still goes to Christ.

When a priest is referred to as 'spiritual father' ('otche duhovny' in Slav), the spiritual fatherhood of God the Father, manifested in Christ the Son is recognised and acknowledged. During the Divine Liturgy of the Byzantine church, the priest or bishop is referred to as 'Lord' or 'Master'; for example, at the beginning of the Liturgy the deacon says: 'Give the Blessing, Master' ('vladyko' in Slav). It is Christ's Lordship that is present iconically in the priest.

Finally, since an icon transmits the gospel message in a pictorial form, the priest, as icon, also transmits, by his priestly actions, the truth of the incarnation and the saving work of Christ. It is by virtue of the ordained priest's maleness that there can be such iconic communication of the knowledge of God. For it is by maleness that Christ, the male High Priest, can be pictorially represented. Women also, of course, are to transmit the knowledge of God to others. This is an imperative of the Christian vocation. Yet she does not do it, she cannot do it, through a *liturgical* iconic relationship to Christ the High Priest, the Head of the Church.

If a woman presumed to seek sacramental ordination to the priesthood, she would not be seeking to represent Christ, the incarnate Logos. She would be seeking a role bereft of a relational identity, such as is found in the icon. The christocentric 'christoiconic' priesthood would be destroyed. Just as with the iconoclast Byzantine emperors, who substituted their own images (on their minted coins) for the image of Christ, so an anthropocentric and 'anthropoiconic' priesthood would

These conclusions, though they may seem harsh to hopes and aspirations of many genuinely spiritual women, follow inexorably from the traditional theology of the eastern (and for that matter western) church. The severity is proportionate to the importance of the priesthood in the church, as found in Tradition and understood in Tradition. Tradition cannot be seen, as many proponents of female ordination see it, as the musty and anachronistic residue of wasted centuries. Tradition, rather, represents the living stream that flows from the Bible, through the Fathers of the Church, into the present day.

All of this does not imply however, that women do not have their own elevated place in the church. We have seen that the contribution of women to the development and growth of the church was recognised from the very beginnings of Christianity, and it is important that this contribution should continue.

Conclusion. The Theotokos and the role of women in the church.

To celebrate the overcoming of the iconoclast heresy the Byzantine church dedicated a special feast called the 'Triumph of Orthodoxy' for the first Sunday of Lent. In the kontakion of the day (a liturgical hymn not dissimilar to the Roman 'collect'), the holy Theotokos is addressed:

'The indefinable word of the Father became circumscribed when he was incarnate in you, O Mother of God, and having refashioned the soiled image to its former estate, has suffused it with divine beauty. But confessing salvation, we show it forth in deed and word.'

It was because of Mary's faithful correspondence to her vocation, and to her place among God's people, that we have all received the divine 'gift' of the Incarnate Son. It is because of the Theotokos that God was made incarnate, and therefore became representable to us. It is because of her that we have an iconically representable High Priest who mediates for us before God the Father. The Theotokos is that indispensible instrument in the 'refashioning of the soiled image' of God in our being. The first iconoclasm, at the time of the fall of Adam and Eve, was the work of the devil. The role of the Theotokos was to co-operate in crushing the power of the Great Iconoclast. It is still her role to prevent any iconoclastic distortion of the roles of Christian men and women in the economy of the Redemption. She is the New Eve who symbolizes feminity in the church, the icon of the role and position of women in the church.[73] Thus there is a clear connection between a correct understanding and veneration of the Blessed Virgin and a correct understanding of the priesthood. Bishop Kallistos Ware has written:

'It is significant that the movement for the ordination of women should first have emerged in those Christian communities that tend to neglect the Holy Virgin's place in Christ's redemptive work.'[74].

Woman's dignity in the church derives from her regeneration in Christ through baptism. Her most elevated task is to strive for sanctity, the clearest model of which among God's creatures is the Holy Virgin.

The ministries of the church are only a small part of the Christian service, that service which is of the essence of the Christian vocation. A woman may be called to a particular public witness to God's truth, through consecrated virginity and even martyrdom. She may be extremely instrumental in spreading God's word: indeed, some of the women saints in the Byzantine Liturgical Calendar have been given the title 'equal to the apostles'.

Yet, like the Theotokos, every women is called to be

totally transfigured by sanctifying grace. She is to become Christ-like, never as a priestly icon, but always in her femininity, her individuality and her uniqueness.

Notes.

1. Whilst this is true, many individual aspects of feminist theology have appeared in history (as we will see below).
2. Thus the Roman Pontiff, John Paul II, issued the encyclical *Mulieris Dignitatem*, 15 August 1988, a meditative exposition of the church's understanding of the role of women in the church.
3. The first official theological dialogue between the Orthodox and Anglican communities took place between 1973-1976. These talks led to the Moscow Agreed Statement of 1976.
4. *Anglican-Orthodox Dialogue*. The Dublin Agreed Statement 1984(SPCK, 1985), 59. (The appendices of this work include the Moscow Agreed Statement of 1976 and the Athens Report of 1978).
5. *Anglican-Orthodox Dialogue*, ibid, 62
6. Vladimir Lossky, *In the Image and Likeness of God* (Crestwood, NY, St. Vladimir's Seminary Press, 1974), 156.
7. Athens Report, n.4 in *Anglican-Orthodox Dialogue,* 60.
8. From the VIIth Ecumenical Council (Nicaea II,787): *Conciliorum Decumenicorum Decreta* (Herder, Bologna, 1962), 135: *. . . walking, so to speak, on the royal road, following the divinely inspired teaching of our Holy Fathers, as well as the Tradition of the Catholic Church (for we know that it belongs to the Holy Spirit which dwells in the Church), we define . . . . .*
9. Moscow Agreed Statement (MAS), n.10: *Anglican-Orthodox Dialogue* 51.
10. MAS, n.9: ibid.
11. MAS n.5: ibid.
12. Reproduced in the appendix.
13. Cf. Deborah Belonick "The Spirit of the Female Priesthood" in *Women and the Priesthood,* ed. Thomas Hopko (Crestwood NY, St. Vladimir's Seminary Press, 1983) 135-168.
14. Dublin Agreed Statement, 1984, n.3: *Anglican-Orthodox Dialogue*, 9.
15. Athens Report 1978, IV 1: *Anglican-Orthodox Dialogue*, 62.
16. Terms used by the Inter-Orthodox Consultation, n.2
17. Inter-Orthodox Consultation, n.2.
18. C.f. Sacred Congregation for the Doctrine of the Faith, *Inter Insigniores* 15 Oct 1976.
19. Inter-Orthodox Consultation, n.4.
20. Hauke also argues that the 'subordination' of women in the Bible is a co-relative term to leadership and does not imply oppression or inferiority. Leadership means service, and if it leads to a superior -inferior relationship, then this is the result of sin. In both the order of

creation and the order or economy of redemption, this service is particularly suited to males. Women have equal dignity with men, being made in the image and likeness of God, but their femininity makes other services particularly appropriate for them. They are not inferior to men, but different from them.

21. The points presented in this section have been taken from Manfred Hauke, *Women in the Priesthood, passim,* but especially pages 404-421.

22. We see here, in an anticipated form, the doctrine found in feminist theology.

23. Cf. Hauke (see above) 158-165.

24. Differences between the sexes were purely biological for the Gnostics.

25. Quotations taken from Hauke (see above) 404-405.

26. Irenaeus, *Contra haereses,* 1,13: *Patrologia Graeca* (PG) 7, 577-593

27. Epiphanius, *Adversus haereses,*49,1-3.PG 41, 880-881.

28. *Adversus haereses,* 49, 1:PG 41, 880d

29. Origen, Commentary on 1 Corinthians 14:35-35: *Journal of Theological Studies* 10 (1909): 41f. Hauke 410.

30. *De Virginibus velandis* 9.1 (This was written when Tertullian was still a montanist).*Patrologia Labina* (PL) 2, 950b

31. Hippolytus, *Traditio Apostolica,* 10.

32. Canones Hippolyti 9: *Patrologia Orientalis* 31.

33. *Inter epistulas Cypriani* 75,10.

34. The Didascalia has the *first* certain reference to this permanent office. The other three references in Christian literature are in Romans 16:1; 1 Timothy 3:11 and the 'ministrae' of Pliny. These, Hauke believes, refer to a welfare 'service' rather than a permanent office: Cf. Hauke 440. An opposing view is given by Kyriaki K. Fitzgerald - 'The characteristics and nature of the order of the Deaconess' in *Women and the Priesthood,* 76-78.

35. *Didascalia,* III, 6, 1-2.

36. *Didascalia,* III, 12:17; 13:1.

37. Ibid, 6:2.

38. *Apostolic Constitutions,* III, 9:3.

39. Ibid; II, 4:26; II, 7:57-8.

40. Ibid; VIII, 28:6,

41. For a more detailed treatment of this subject, cf Hauke, 440-440 and the authors he refers to, especially Gryson and Martimort.

42. *Apostolic Church Order,* 24:1-28,1.

43. Epiphanius, *Adversus haereses* 78:23. PG 42, 736b-c.

44. *Adversus haereses* 79:2. PG 42, 744a.

45. Ibid; 79:3. PG 42, 744b.

46. Ibid; 79:1,2. PG 42, 741a-b; cf. 736b

47. *Adversus haereses:* 79.3 PG 42, 744c-d.

48. Hauke (see above), 418.

49. John Chrysostom, *De Sacerdotio,* 2,2. PG 48, 633.

50. Hauke, 419.

51. Alexander Schmemann, *Introduction to Liturgical Worship* (St. Vladmimir's Seminary Press, Crestwood, NY 1986), 29.

52. Dublin Agreed Statement, ns 53 & 54; *Anglican-Orthodox Dialogue* 30-31.

53. Discourse 19 on the Forty Martyrs, PG 32, 509a.

54. St. Basil the Great, *On the Holy Spirit* 18: PG 32, 149c.

55. Cf. Leonid Ouspensky in L. Ouspensky, V. Lossky, *The Meaning of Icons* (St. Vladmimir's Seminary Press, Crestwood, New York 1982), 30-31.

56. *Conciliorum Oec. Decreta*, 135.

57. L. Ouspensky, ibid, 30.

58. Seventh Ecumenical Council: *Conc. Oec.Decreta*, 136.

59. Elizabeth Behr-Sigel, 'The participation of women in the life of the church', in Ion Bria ed. *Martyria/Mission: The Witness of the Orthodox Churches Today* (Geneva 1980), 59.

60. *On Holy Icons* 1:16; PG 94, 1245b.

61. For a fuller discussion of this topic and the ramifications of the doctrine of Nicaea II, see John Saward, *Christ, Our Lord and the Church in the Teaching of the Second Council of Nicaea* in *Chrysostom* (Special number), Vol VIII n.1, 1988.

62. Theodore Studite, *Antirrheticus* III, 1, 18, PG 99, 397c.

63. Saward, *Christ Our Lady and the Church*, 13.

64. Ibid, 13-14,

65. Cf. Ibid, 15.

66. Theodore Studite, *Seven Chapters against the Iconoclasts* Chapter 4, PG 99, 945c.

67. *To the Magnesians* 6:1; Cf. *To the Trallians* 3,1; *To the Smyreans* 8.1.

68. Dionysius Pseudo Areopagite, *The Ecclesiastical Hierarchy* III, 13. PG 3, 444c.

69. Germanus of Constantinople, *Ecclesiastical History and Mystical Contemplation*, n.26 PG 98, 409c.

70. Joseph Lecuyer, *Le Sacrement de l'ordination* Recherche historique et theologique (Paris 1983), passim.

71. St. Bonaventure *In IV Sent.*, d. 25, a.2.q.1; St. Thomas Aquinas, ST 3a, 83, 1 ad 3.

72. Nicaea II: *Conciliorum Oecumenicorum Decreta* (Bologna 1973), 136.

73. Cf. Paul Evdokimov, *Woman and the Salvation of the World* (in German) (Munich, 1960), 237f.

74. *Man, Woman and the Priesthood of Christ*, in *Women and the Priesthood*, op. cit., 22.

Reflections of Feminism and Christianity

Mary Kenny

The institutions of religion in general, and the Judeo-Christian tradition in particular, have certainly taken a hammering from feminists in recent years. While women are, by common and universal observation, consistantly more religious in practice than men are, the institutions of religions have been condemned as being merely part of a male "system" which exploits and manipulates women. "A religion created by men, for men," was how the English feminist Eva Figes described Christianity, though she herself is Jewish: quite apt, indeed, since Jewish feminists are often even more ferocious about the religion *they* have created by men for men. Much of the animus of the feminist movement in America has come from clever Jewish girls who felt undervalued by the religious background in which they grew up-Betty Friedan, Gloria Steinem, Andrea Dworkin, Shulamith Firestone-or, perhaps, the Jewish values which were simply transmitted to them by unconscious cultural osmosis. But Judaism and Christianity are intertwined, root and branch, and begin with the same story in the Garden of Eden: Women in the feminist movements have bitterly resented what they have termed the "framing" of Eve, right from the start. *She* was made to take the rap for the Fall of Mankind-or, as we have been asked to say, humankind.

"The woman did tempt me, and I did eat." The story
of Adam and Eve in the Garden of Paradise is, of course,
a very significant one. The feminists are right to take it
seriously, because it represents the truth of our fallen
state, our imperfect and flawed nature. What they take
seriously, too, is the detail in the story about Eve being
made from Adam's rib. The inferior status of women is
thus traced mythically, anyway, back to Eve, the
mother of our miseries ("Frailty, thy name is
woman!"). As a consequence, too, of having been
created as a second thought, to keep Adam company, as
it were, Eve may well be viewed as being second best.
Of course, people see the story differently, and some
women in the Church are keen to point out the
symbolic value of Eve having been created from
Adam's *side* (rather than from, say, his little finger): in
this way, was God making the point that Eve was a
side-by-side companion, rather than an inferior second-
string?

Actually, it is extremely difficult to wriggle out of the
accusation that the Bible is male chauvinist. Let's face it:
it is. Certainly, the Old Testament has a fundamentalist-
it would have, wouldn't it?-approach to the position of
Male and Female. Still and all, you have to take all these
matters in the context of their time and of the evolution
of history. In ancient times, Katharine Moore tells us,
"hunting and warfare and the ceaseless struggle for
feeding-grounds were the determining factors of existence. Women and children were a burden in such a way
of life: so many mouths to feed and no use in battle.
Abraham belonged to a nomadic pastoral people and the
Mosaic law, as it took shape, favoured men. Jaweh, the
Jewish god, is unmistakeably and uncompromisingly
masculine and alone among the gods he had no
consort." There is a fond feminist mythology that there
once existed an ancient Utopia when the Earth-Mother
ruled the universe, and all was sweetness and light: but

most well-chronicled ancient societies were brutally male chauvinist, whether in the savage fight for existence among nomadic tribes like the Jews, or the homophilec misogyny of ancient Greece. Anyone who witnesses modern history can also witness human reversals to this ruthless male chauvinism linked to survival: during the Biafra war in 1967, my husband was appalled to see that under siege, babies and women were allowed to die, while the young men were all given the good rations. Why, he asked, still erroneously thinking like a European Christian in whom the chivalric tradition of "women and children first" still lingered. Because, he was told, young men fight. Young men defend the territory. The young men who defend the territory get priority. It is like lions at feeding time; the male always get to eat first. It is like the tradition of the *shaman-hunter* among certain Arctic peoples. On the skill of the leading hunter the survival of the whole clan may depend: therefore *he* gets priority. Certain aspects of what we call male chauvinism are merely survival techniques. Yet male chauvinism is also primitive, and closer to animal behaviour. In nature, it is obvious that the male (for the most part) is dominant because he can fertilise so many females; though paradoxically, because only one male is required for every hundred females (among, say, the antelope), he is also more expendable in numbers, especially once his reproductive role has been completed.

Dominant patterns of behaviour also exist in human males–as a cursory examination of modern anthropology will confirm–but so, of course, does the expendibility of the male, who hardly ever lives as long as the female, and still remains more vulnerable to disease and accidents than she.

As society evolves into more complex and sophisticated patterns, it may develop a more reflective and dignified attitude to the female: although not invariably, of course. Many societies which developed culture and civilisation remained male chauvinist, especially if, like Rome, they were essentially warrior societies. Still, it is accepted that the advent of Christianity initially certainly meant an advance for women. In the gospels, Jesus treats women seriously, in an amicable way, and as intellectual equals. The story of Martha and Mary seems to indicate that Jesus thought it quite okay for women to prefer theological discussion to pot-walloping in the kitchen: those of us who do not relish household chores always appreciate that one. Jesus's defence of Mary Magdalene and of the woman taken in adultery is an evolutionary step which certain middle Eastern societies, where the stoning of adulteresses is still practised, have still not matched. It is generally considered to be significant that women featured strongly in the agony of the crucifixion, and women were the first witnesses of the Resurrection. Women were active and highly visible among the early Christians and from the very beginning, indeed, Christianity had a unique appeal for women. Indeed, Ameury de Riencourt tells us, it was mostly under feminine influence that men were converted to Christianity.

"High-ranking women and female members of the imperial households were often converts to Christianity, who attempted to induce their husbands, fathers, brothers, to join them in the new faith.... Both Diocletian's wife and daughter were strongly inclined towards the new faith. Emperor Constantine's mother, Flavia Helena, wife of Constantius Chlorus, had great powers of persuasion: in 313 he put an end to the persecution of Christianity...." Moreover, it was feminine influence under Christian leadership which also dissolved some of the most partriarchal and cruel of Roman marital laws, which had discriminated so emphatically against women.

The Christianised marital laws of Rome brought a

new balance: what was licit now was licit for both sexes; and what was forbidden now was forbidden to both sexes.

It is widely agreed that Christianity was initially an advance for women, even though St Paul - being a Hellenised Jew, and therefore inheritor of two male chauvinist traditions - remained sternly patriarchal in his preaching. But the Christian idea was - and remained - deeply attractive to women. Christian missionaries in the Third World to this day make their strongest appeal first to the womenfolk of any given non-Christian area, for in many parts of the world still a woman advances her status by becoming a Christian. (Just as in India, people who oppressed by the *caste* system find a welcoming sense of "equality in the sight of the Lord" within Christianity.)

Where the radical criticisms of Christian male chauvinism are directed at the early fathers of the Church, who were, indeed, well, patriarchal. Tertullian, St Ambrose, St Justin and St Jerome are often quoted for their harsh views of female sexuality. "Woman! you are the gateway to the devil.... A woman is a temple built over a sewer!" (Tertullian.) There seemed to be a great deal of what the Freudians would call *projection* by these early church fathers. If St Jerome saw dancing girls before his mind's eye when he retired to the desert to pray, he blamed it not on his own desires, but, bewilderingly, on the fantasy girls. Again, however, this notion of woman as temptress and as the source of the lust that men feel was not something that the early saints plucked out of the blue, just as the taboo against menstruation was not, with respect, something that Judeo-Christians just thought up in order to be disobliging. These ideas persisted in many cultures, and have a certain universality. There is a tendency among writers especially to blame what is general on the particular. The notion that women are sex objects and send the blood of young men racing faster is neither Jewish nor Christian nor Catholic nor Protestant: but extraordinarily universal. The idea that mothers-in-law are uniquely vexatious to Lancashire comedians who have a tradition of making jokes about them is fallacious: the mother-in-law joke (and fear) is universal. The observation that women make a fuss of their sons, worry about what they eat, and are possessive about who they consort with, is not a social phenomenon limited to the experience of Jewish American novelists: it happens from Bali to Ballybunion. Certain early Christian fathers had crude ideas about women and their sexual temptations, but they were not the only ones. *There was a lot of it about.* And sometimes, it had to be said, the strong-minded mothers of these early Christian chaps were the very ones who had inspired their Christianity in the first place. Ambrose, Jerome, Gregory the Great and of course Augustine all testified that their mothers were the strongest influence on their lives. This was also the case for many of the Eastern Church Fathers–Athanasius, Basil of Caesarea, Gregory of Nazianzus, John of Damascus all paid homage to the Christian leadership of their mothers. (The influence of women in early charitable works was also a source of much edification.)

Could it have been that these early Church fathers, who were so thoroughly prudish about sex, were actually encouraged to make these attitudes by the women in their lives–their mothers? It could easily have been. And could it have been that the women to whom they preached actually approved of all this "repression"? It is very likely so.

Clerics like Bishop Jack Spong, the liberal American Episcopalian, excoriate the Christian church for impart-

ing so much "guilt" towards sexuality. But look at it
this way. The early Christians were reacting vividly
against the decadence and excesses of the Roman
Empire in its decline. They loathed what the permissive
society of the time had done to the appetites of men-and
I mean *men*-and how this licentiousness had exploited
women and debauched young people. They saw how
unhappy lasciviousness made people and how much it
attacked the basis of society. In their prudishness, the
early Christians gained the approval of women, for the
mothers of Saints Ambrose, Jerome and Gregory were,
in a way, the Mary Whitehouses of their day: decent
Christian women who thought all this porn had got
way out of hand.

Women often welcome the disciplining of men's
sexual impulses-which, in nature are everywhere more
prodigious than the female's-and Christian women
undoubtedly welcomed the restraints which Christianity imposed on men. And just as there were a few Mary
Whitehouses around to check the excesses of sexual
licence, so there would have been a few Mandy
Rice-Davies, too. St Jerome may have protested somewhat, but no doubt he had been provoked by the odd
little trollope, too. This scenario is only human, as well
as being animal.

Throughout the developing Christian era, Christianity
went on being a religion that women related to
particularly well, and in which women expressed their
own spirituality fulsomely. The dictionaries of the
saints tell us of the many great and holy women who
inspired spiritual and sometimes temporal leadership:
Bertha of Kent, Brigid of Kildare, Etheldreda, Ethelburga, Aethelrith and Cuthberg, Hilda of York, Abbess
Eadburg of Thanet, Abbess Bugga of Kent, Abbess
Eangith of Durham, St Mildred, St Margaret, St Clare
of Assisi, Mother Juliana of Norwich, St Bathild, St
Bridget of Sweden, St Colette, St Catherine of Sienna,

St Elizabeth of Hungary, St Isobel of Portugal, Abbess
Frideswide, St Margery Kempe, St Germaine of Pibrac,
St Godelive, St Hildegard, St Joan of Arc, St Joaquina,
St Jane-Frances de Chantal, St Teresa of Avila...to take
but a few, stretching from the Saxon period until the
eve of the Reformation. The Reformation, or the
Protestant Revolution–as the Marxists call it–certainly
did alter the way in which women were perceived, and
did alter women's lives and choices.

The tradition of devotion to the Virgin Mary had
existed since the beginning of Christianity; and indeed,
some Christian shrines and holy places dedicated to Our
Lady appeared in similar locations to where, formerly, a
female goddess (particularly of fertility) had been
worshipped. The heady years of mariology were
between the 13th and 15th centuries, when the de-
votional shrines to the B.V.M. sprang up so copiously,
and saints like Bonaventure and St Simon Stock
experienced visions of the Madonna, and St Bernard of
Claytaux spread the recitation of the Rosary. The great
feasts of Our Lady–Feast of the Presentation (established
1372), Feast of the Visitation (est. 1389) Feast of Our
Lady of Dolours (est. 1423), Angelus prayer introduced
(1300–1400), Confraternity on the Rosary (1475) started
in these years. Devotion to the Virgin Mary coincided
with some of the most beautiful and tender paintings,
usually featuring Mary, that exist to this day in
European art: and not coincidentally, the Age of
Chivalry was ushered in on the coat-tails of respect for
the Mother of Jesus.

Chivalry is today greatly despised in modernist and
feminist thinking–it is seen as a form of patronising
behaviour to an inferior or a weakling–but again, within
the context of the evolution of Western civilisation, I
think it must be understood as historically progressive.
We may still visit a society which evolved, say, under
Turkish rule: take a country like Albania. Here we can

see, still, the man of the household riding on a donkey, while the womenfolk walk behind. The chivalrous, Western Christian idea of treating women more gently surely *is* an advance to that of some other societies, which persistently treated women more harshly. (Edith Durham the traveller, chronicles how, in the Turkanised Balkans in the late 19th century, women were widely regarded as being of less value than a good horse.) Personally speaking, if there is a choice between being treated chivalrously, of being given the privilege of "women and children first" when the Titanics are sinking, or, alternatively, of walking ten paces behind an Albanian on an ass, I would like to put it on the record that I would prefer the chivalry treatment. And any woman who doesn't prefer chivalry deserves to walk behind an Albanian on his ass.

However, the age of mariology was also, to some extent, the age of mariolotry, and undoubtedly, devotions sometimes spilled into superstitions, and indulgences were sold for fiscal returns. The Protestant revolution was indeed justified in some quarters. It did bring about some much-needed reforms, though the price to be paid was a split church, and a further fissuring of Christianity which has gone on to this day. It also put women firmly back into the home, closing up the convents and the great institutions of prayer and learning which the abbesses managed. "All the Magisterial Reformed Churches stressed the subordination of wives to husbands," the historian Lawrence Stone writes, "summed up in John Milton's terse description of sex-typed obligations: 'He for God only, she for God in him'." Luther believed that "Women should remain at home, sit still, keep house and bear and bring up children." Calvin and John Knox were sternly inclined to the same view.

The Protestant view of marriage did, in the end, enhance the institution of marriage; the Protestant

virtues of cultivating domestic arts and making the
home a place of serenity and Christian order were also
fundamentally civilizing. It especially paid off in the
19th century when slums and degrading alcoholism
were socially linked with domestic squalor, and, *par
contre*, marriage, sobriety and domesticity countered
these social ills. Yet in the 16th and 17th centuries, the
closing of the convents was a great step backwards for
women. Cloisters could, of course, be abused–anything
can be abused–but the institution of the convent
provided an alternative life and choice for women who
did not wish to marry, women who not only felt called
to prayer, but often also felt called to scholarship and
study. "In 1548," writes Stone, "John Udall proudly
drew Queen Catherine Parr's attention to 'the great
number of noble women at that time in England not
only given to the study of humane sciences and strange
tongues, but also so thoroughly expert in Holy Scriptures that they were able to compare with the best
writers'." These learned women, schooled by the
teachers and tutors of the male and female religious,
spoke Latin and Greek, French and Italian, studied the
sciences and the humanities. The Protestant reformers
thought that women had no role outside of marriage
and the home and put an end to such scholarship. Not
coincidentally, the cult of the Virgin Mary was at the
same time severely curtailed in the lands of the
Reformed faith.

Nevertheless, Christianity continued, one way and
another, to be a faith in which women found a means of
expressing their inner and outer selves. If some forms of
Protestantism initially restricted women, other forms
produced new opportunities for women. From the
start, the Quakers took the prescription that "There can

be no male and female, for ye are all one in Jesus Christ" seriously. The founder of Quakerism, George Fox, preached equality of the sexes from 1647. Quakerism soon produced remarkable women missionaries–Margaret Fell, Barbara Blangdone, Mary Fisher, and of course the great prison reformer, Elizabeth Fry. And once into the 18th century, we begin to see the seeds of modern feminism, which were frequently linked with Christian evangelism. Hannah More, the Wesleyan evangelist, referred to as "a Bishop in Petticoats", was also the archetype of the feminist bluestocking. In the 19th century, feminism and Christianity often went hand in hand: Florence Nightingale, Catherine Booth, Josephine Butler, Susan Anthony, Caroline Chisholm, Elizabeth Cady Stanton were all seen as crusading Christian feminists. Not infrequently, Christian feminism also went with temperance, and with anti–slavery. Within the Roman Catholic tradition, women's energies tended to move towards founding convents for the education of girls and there is no doubt that the women who founded the missionary orders too – like Mother Mary Aikenhead-or the teaching orders-Mother Catherine McAulcy-were remarkable, strong, purposeful women who, by every reasonable measure would qualify for the title of feminist.

Of course, in the late 19th century, a more secular form of feminism also began to flourish, feminism which targeted political rights. There were two forms of this secular feminism. One was expressed through the Suffragette movement in England, which was fierce in some of its forms of expression, but upright, correct, highly prudish, and fundamentally, as it turned out, basically conservative. The second influence of secular feminism was to be the more significant, and this was the feminism which grew out of German socialism and British trade unionism: a feminism of the Left which linked greater personal right with political rights.

Perhaps Rosa Luxembourg is the examplar of this strain. The German Socialist-feminists believed in birth control, even in abortion rights, long before these ideas were respectable in Britain. Indeed, the birth control campaign started by Marie Stopes was initially much more widely supported by men than women, for it was men, rather more than women, who were keen on controlling their fertility.

Feminism ebbed and flowed throughout the first half of the twentieth century because again, we must see it in the context of its time; after the First World War, the daughters of the Edwardian blue-stockings turned around and became flappers, and although serious blue-stockinged girls began to come down from Oxford and Cambridge with first-class degrees and the Bloomsbury classes continued in the exercise of their intellectualised forms of feminist discourse, the 1920s was not a decade much concerned with the feminist wave. Birth control rights gradually expanded in the thirties, as did demands for legislation for abortion-a legalisation which took place in several Scandinavian countries. It is widely believed that this would have occurred in Britain, too, by 1940 if the Second World War had not intervened.

Wars notoriously give women more opportunties to enter areas of the work force previously regarded as a male preserve, and both World Wars did this. Many of the seeds of the feminist revolution of the 1960s and 70s were sown in the 1940s, when creches were set up for working mums, when women enjoyed a wave of personal and sexual freedom, and when Princess Elizabeth-as the Queen then was-was photographed changing the wheel of a jeep. However, post-war periods are notoriously pro-natalist. Men and women seem to be overcome by the urge to go home and make babies. There is a theory that more boys are born after a war, as though nature *knew* it had to compensate for the loss of males. There is also a well-observed practice that a period of quietism follows a war. We look back on the 1950s now as dull and conformist, yet this mood seemed precisely what people required after the *bouleversements* and displacements of World War II.

Then the late 1960s produced the contemporary wave of feminism. At first, the women's revolution began alongside(and was conflated with) the sexual revolution. The oral contraceptive came on the market in 1961 and gave people the feeling that, in the words of Hugh Hefner, founder of the Playboy Empire, "procreation could now be replaced by recreation". Sex as play was to replace sex as transmission of life. That was the theory; but human behaviour seldom sticks to theory, and as contraception spread, so did the abortion figures. Abortion was legalized in Britain in 1967, hailed at the time as a great step for women-although men in general always have been and still are more pro-abortion than women- and, moreover, a herald of better times. It was believed that with the increasing availability of contraception, abortion on demand would fall (it was at about 14,000 annually in 1967-68). In fact, it has risen every single year since legalization, and is now at about 188,000 annually.

However, the feminist revolution was not exactly the same as the sex revolution, although both have been neatly exploited by commercial media like Cosmopolitan magazine as though they existed in tandem. They do not. An interesting area of observation lies in the subject of pornography. In the 1960s and up to the middle 1970s, feminism was siding with liberalism in opposing "censorship" at all costs. But by the late 1970s, feminism had begun to revert to some of its traditional moralizing roots by deploring the rise of violent pornography and the use of women's bodies as "sex objects" in advertising or casual entertainment and titillation. By 1988, the left-wing feminist M.P. Clare

Short was seeking to introduce a Private members' Bill in the House of Commons to ban "Page Three" nudist pin-ups in the newspapers of Mr Rupert Murdoch.

In discussing Ms. Short's Bills, the old-style anti-censorship libertarians were emphatically opposed to the feminists. But then again the wider issue of pornography had begun to unite women who were, again, previously opposed: by 1988, Mary Whitehouse was winning university debates on the pornography issue, largely because she was now being supported by the boiler-suited feminist brigade, who, tattoos on arms and rings in noses, were clench-fisting Mrs Whitehouse with a "Right on, Mary!" sisterly salute. (Ah, Judy O'Grady and the Colonel's lady are sisters under the skin!)

Feminism has fissured and diversified - rather as Protestantism did before it. It has also achieved an astonishing success in a relatively short period of time. It is a very adaptable issue, in a way, for a woman may be a feminist and a Conservative, a feminist and a Socialist, a feminist and an Ecologist, or Peace-Movementer (a strong tradition there), whatever. The one constituency that feminism tends to omit (although this was never intended) is that of the housewife. There is not a lot of feminism around for the woman who chooses to remain at home. But then it is not a popular choice these days, either with the Left or the Right. The Left has traditionally been strong on women in the workforce anyhow; and the Right - well, the Right desperately wants more married women in the work-force for the 1990s, because capitalism is about to suffer an acute shortage of skilled staff. As with abortion (where both the extreme Left and the extreme libertarian Right have combined to crush the dissenters who worry about the choice available to the fetus), the more traditional ground is quickly being sealed off as a no-go area. Much of modern feminism has, of course, been extremely materialistic, with its emphasis on equal pay, taxation rights, division of the matrimonial property after divorce, and so on. But lo and behold, what is the latest passion to grip feminism? Why, the passionate desire to be ordained for the priesthood.

I do not know enough about theology to make any judgement about the suitability of women for the priesthood; I would rather revert to muttering old Vatican saws about the wisdom of thinking in centuries. Give it time, I say.

Yet there is one aspect of the controversy that I consider positive and significant. These holy women who desire to serve in a ministry must, in a way, be four-square in the tradition of the great abbesses, of St Etheldreda and St Ethelburga, of St Catherine and St Hilda. In a sense, the turning of women towards the church is a turning away from the crass materialism of some of the 1970s feminism-is it not? If they want to be priests, then at least they must be interested in spirituality, in the pursuit of goodness, in the moral ideas that Christian women have concerned themselves with since the beginning of Christianity.

Yet, things are a lot less simple than in the days of St Ita and St Bathild: Christian women in past times certainly were headstrong in the service of God (St Jane de Chantal walking out on her family in order to found the Visitation Nuns, despite her children's pleas to stay at home); they were controversial and went against the Church establishment. Even St Bernadette of Lourdes had to run the gauntlet of male disapproval in the hierarchy, after all. ("How could a little illiterate peasant girl know better than us learned men!") But Christian women in the past were clear about substance and objectives, which were to save your own soul, and then to save the soul of others, broadly. Today, I do not believe we are at all clear about either objectives or substance. There are many muddles within Christianity, and there is one major muddle within contemporary Christian feminism: the major muddle is simply that feminism itself has not been able to decide whether it aims for equality with men because men and women are basically the same, or whether women should have special treatment from men, because men and women are basically different. For example, the deaconess who came on Panorama on BBC television in April 1988 and said that the only difference between her and the vicar was that the vicar had a penis-she presumably subscribes to the theory that men and women are the same, give or take a couple of genital and reproductive details. But feminists like Dr Marietta Higgs-a Catholic, by the way-who campaign so ferociously against child abuse definitely do not believe that men and women are basically the same. They believe that child-abusers are men and hardly ever women, and there is a huge difference between the two genders. The feminists who campaign, now, against porn and against the ever-rising tide of rape have moved away from the unisex view of men and women-"the-only-difference-is-a-penis" idea. And if men and women are deeply and fundamentally different, then how exactly can they be equal? Only, perhaps, in the sight of God.

Moreover, the "equalitarian" view of men and women tends to become, in reality, a *masculine* view of men and women. It boils down, in a way, to the old Greek notion that basically, all people are men, or should be men. I am aware of the campaign to make church language "inclusive", so that in effect it replaces references of "mankind" with "humanity", and even "Father" to "Parent" ("Our Parent who art in Heaven..."). But that, I feel, is cosmetic and will fail largely because it is seeking to replace beautiful, specific language with banal, generalized language: and anyone who thinks they should re-write the hymns of Charles Wesley in order to make them less sexist should be burnt at the stake, in effigy at least. Yet I am struck, again and again, by the thinking of some of the ordination-for-women lobby, that it is, so often, deeply male chauvinist. For example, it so often seems merely to brush aside motherhood as an irrelevance, or just as another "private choice", like preferring tea to coffee. Jennifer Chapman, in her book on women's ordination, refers in passing to "the social handicap of childbearing". Social handicap! Speak for yourself, sister! It may be a "social handicap" to *you*: to me, it is an estimable privilege, besides which the riches of the Bank of England or the tea accumulated in China stand at naught. Bishop Spong writes about childbearing in exactly the same tone as Hugh Hefner, who separated "procreation" from "recreation" all those permissive years ago. "Now that conception has been safely separated from sexual activity...." he writes, displaying a dismaying lack of understanding of the psychology of women. If only he had the sense and the sensibility of an agnostic, non-Christian writer like Irma Kurtz, and if only he would apply himself to read her book about men, *Malespeak*. There he would see it spelled out, with an understanding no recent theologian seems to have reached, the profound, the truly awe-ful differences between the psycho-sexual characters of men and women, and how it is that for the majority of women, sexual activity and conception can *never* be separated in their hearts. "Sooner or later," she writes, "most men want to start a family, and a little bit sooner women want to have babies." Parturition is a mystery of life which is closed to men. For men, sex is a performance, a spilling of seed: for women the sex is the seed, but always, at some level of the unconscious mind, the baby is the harvest. To dismiss motherhood (as Spong does)

as a biological function - as though it were *just* a
biological function, like the working of the intestines or
the sleeping rhythms of the brain, is to miss the
tremendous drama that is motherhood, and that is so
tumultuous in the lives of most women. Motherhood is
not the same as fatherhood, and never can be: there are
no unisex rights on the agenda here, not now or ever.
Motherhood is simply infinitely more important. The
unisex lobby, because it is masculine in its inspiration-
because, in Jung's sense, it is inspired by the *animus* and
not the *anima,* disregards motherhood, or brushes it
aside. The ordained American woman, the Rev Lesley
Northrup, who inseminated herself with sperm from
three different donors and brought forth a "sperm gift'
baby in December 1987, drew the wrath of the
feminist-christians for bringing the cause into disrepute,
if not into ridicule, but in achieving motherhood she at
least was following the true instinct of a woman, rather
more, indeed, than those women who wish to replace
men as priests.

'There are aspects of the ordination of women for
which I have sympathy, because there is a spiritual
element in the movement; in the end it is holiness that
counts, and if that is there, one is willing to believe that
the Holy Spirit is leading us on. But I remain cautious
about the unisex aspect of such thinking, because unisex
thinking misunderstands the feelings and the profound
differences betwen men and women, and can, moreover
distort and deform them. The Bishop of London drew
great sneers from the movement for women's ordination when he said that when faced with a woman in
charge of an altar "my instinct would be to take her in
my arms... human sexuality is built into human life and
you cannot get rid of it." The "equalitarians" replied
that, after all, women had almost certainly lusted after
dishy curates for years: this reply was made *as if the
sexuality of men and women were the same.* But it is well

established that it is *not* the same. Women do not rape, create a demand for brothels, fetish-shops, or fill the case-book pages of Kraft-Ebbing. Women do not demand "Page Three" boys over which to masturbate; and if "Page Three" boys did start appearing in tabloid newspapers, they would attract not women, but gay men. The Bishop of London is factually right in making a distinction between the sexuality of men and the sexuality of women: a woman on any platform is more of a sex-object: every woman with a public role, from Margaret Thatcher to Joan Collins, is the object of some man's rape fantasy. That is not true of every male public figure. The sexes are different.

I am cautious about the women-as-priests lobby *not* on theological grounds-because I am not competent to judge, here - but on the instinctive hunch that it is an urge which comes from the animus: that it is another area in which some women want to ape men, rather than develop their own female nature. Wherever "unisex" models have developed, in the secular world, women have simply become more like men - dressing like men, living like men, acting like men. Among career women, who live male-like lives, the diseases of men catch up with them, as do the social vices of men: more and more career women drink like men, for instance, even though the physiological fact is that women's livers are very substantially less resilient to alcohol-abuse than those of men. But to me, apeing men and developing the values of men is not real feminism; it is not in the interests of women, that is. Some of the things that are good for men are very bad for women. Divorce (which again, Bishop Spong, claims can be a very positive thing) is an area of divergence worthy of study. American feminists are now increasingly pointing out that after divorce, the income of men tends to rise; and the income of women tends to fall. Divorce is causing what is called, now, "the feminization of poverty". Therefore, were the Church's strictures on divorce more in the interests of men, or of women?

The permissive society, and certainly the porn society, both were, as we now know, very much in the interests of men, who, everywhere are more promiscuous than women, a characteristic that Nature, to some degree, has saddled them with. (Regard again the habits of the antelope: he is propelled, as though programmed by nature, to spill his genes as far and wide as possible. Men are not antelopes, but they do produce millions of sperm, where women only produce one monthly egg.)

Personally, I respect male priests because I genuinely believe that it is harder for men to be good, because nature has made men more delinquent (a look at the comparative figures between male and female offenders will confirm this). Because it is harder for men to achieve virtue, and because they can never achieve motherhood, I think, in the final analysis, there is perhaps a reason why the priesthood should be a special sacramental role for men. When I was a child in Ireland, we used to give priests special treats: we brought out the best linen when they came to tea, and the best sherry was produced for the priest's *aperitif*. Priests were encouraged to enjoy the pleasures of the table, and indeed the racecourse: Irish priests still visit Cheltenham Races enthusiastically, I am glad to say. And the reason for all this plying the priest with little privileges was this sense of sacrifice which underlined his role: *because he has given up so much*. Perhaps, when it comes to discussing the gender-roles of the priesthood, it is necessary to look again at celibacy, too. Perhaps, in the long run, celibacy is a greater issue than gender. I think I can see how a priest could be a woman more easily than I could see how a priest could be a mother.

Personal taste does come into all this: some may call it

prejudice: I, having much experience of life try not to pre-judge anything, but nonetheless, I claim preferences. At 45 years of age, you are allowed to have preferences. I do not mind married pastors, but I prefer a celibate priesthood: I make a difference, there, between the sacramental and the non-sacramental role. In the sacramental role, personal sacrifice seems to me to be necessary. I do not much care for unisex roles: I do not appreciate women apeing men-I find the notion of female coal-miners repellant, and a degradation of women-and I am not impressed by the counter-claims that men can ape women. When it comes to priests or pastors, I prefer the robust Irishman who has played football and stood his round of whiskey to the pretty characters in liturgical lace with soft, girlish voices. Men may have to be kept in line occasionally, but they may still be men for all that. (I repeat: I am 45 and I am allowed to have personal preferences.)

It is certain that, as Carl Jung tells us, religion needs both a male and a female component, and these must be kept in balance. I think it is very likely that some of the impetus for a female clergy comes from a sense of loss of the feminine in spirituality; a sense of loss directly related to the decline in devotion to Our Lady - indeed, among some folk, a contempt for the Mother of God because of her purity. It has been well observed that in popular iconography, the more that Mary is put into the background, the more Jesus is portrayed as an effeminate - because the feminine is then being sought in Jesus. On the other hand, the stronger and more vivid that Mary is, as a woman, the more that Jesus is seen as the Man. Historically, after all, even in the atheistic Soviet encyclopaedias, Jesus Christ was undoubtedly a Man, and all the unisex theology in the world cannot define Jesus merely as a Person: God may be a pure spirit, but Jesus was undoubtedly a bloke. Spiritually, male and female may well be intermingled, but as the word was made flesh, *la différence* was there from the start.

APPENDIX

Church Documents relating to Women in the Priesthood

1. *Inter Insigniores*: Sacred Congregation for the Doctrine of the Faith, 15 October 1976
2. Anglican–Orthodox Joint Doctrinal Commission, Athens, July 1978
3. *Baptism, Eucharist and Ministry*: Ministry - paragraphs 15–18, World Council of Churches, 1982
4. Correspondence between the Archbishop of Canterbury and Pope John Paul II, August–December 1988
5. Apostolic Letter, *Mulieris Dignitatem* of Pope John Paul II, paragraphs 23–27, 15 August 1988
6. Inter-Orthodox Theological Consultation on the Place of Women in the Orthodox Church and the Question of the Ordination of Women, paragraphs 1–7, Rhodos, 30 October–7 November 1988
7. The Archbishop of Canterbury's Commission Report: *Koinonia and Women in the Episcopate* - Section III, 1989

Declaration on the admission of Women to the Ministerial Priesthood

S.D.F., Inter insigniores, 15 October, 1976

INTRODUCTION
The role of women in modern society and the Church

Among the characteristics that mark our present age, Pope John XXIII indicated, in his Encyclical *Pacem in Terris* of 11 April 1963, "The part that women are now taking in public life . . .This is a development that is perhaps of swifter growth among Christian nations, but it is also happening extensively, if more slowly, among nations that are heirs to different traditions and imbued with a different culture".[1] Along the same lines, the Second Vatican Council, enumerating in its Pastoral Constitution *Gaudium et Spes* the forms of discrimination touching upon the basic rights of the person which must be overcome and eliminated as being contrary to God's plan, gives first place to discrimination based upon sex.[2] The resulting equality will secure the building up of a world that is not levelled out and uniform but harmonious and unified, if men and women contribute to it their own resources and dynamism, as Pope Paul VI recently stated.[3]

In the life of the Church herself, as history shows us, women have played a decisive role and accomplished tasks of outstanding value. One has only to think of the foundresses of the great religious families, such as Saint Clare and Saint Teresa of Avila. The latter, moreover, and Saint Catherine of Siena, have left writings so rich in spiritual doctrine that Pope Paul VI has included them among the Doctors of the Church. Nor could one forget the great number of women who have consecrated themselves to the Lord for the exercise of charity or for the missions, and the Christian wives who have had a profound influence on their families, particularly for the passing on of the faith to their children.

But our age gives rise to increased demands: "Since in our time women have an ever more active share in the whole life of society, it is very important that they participate more widely also in the various sectors of the Church's apostolate".[4] This charge of the Second Vatican Council has already set in motion the whole process of change now taking place: these various experiences of course need to come to maturity. But as Pope Paul VI also remarked,[5] a very large number of Christian communities are already benefitting from the apostolic commitment of women. Some of these women are called to take part in councils set up for pastoral reflection, at the diocesan or parish level; and the Apostolic See has brought women into some of its working bodies.

For some years now various Christian communities stemming from the sixteeth-century Reformation or of later origin have been admitting women to the pastoral office on a par with men. This initiative has led to petitions and writings by members of these communities and similar groups, directed towards making this admission a general thing; it has also led to contrary reactions. This therefore constitutes an ecumenical problem, and the Catholic Church must make her thinking known on it, all the more because in various sectors of opinion the question has been asked whether she too could not modify her discipline and admit women to priestly ordination. A number of Catholic theologians have even posed this question publicly, evoking studies not only in the sphere of exegesis, patrology and Church history but also in the field of the history of institutions and customs, of sociology and of psychology. The various arguments capable of clarifying this important problem have been submitted to a critical examination. As we are dealing with a debate which classical theology scarcely touched upon, the current argumentation runs the risk of neglecting essential elements.

For these reasons, in execution of a mandate received from the Holy Father and echoing the declaration which he himself made in his letter of 30 November 1975,[6] the Sacred Congregation for the Doctrine of the Faith judges it necessary to recall that the Church, in fidelity to the example of the Lord, does not consider herself authorized to admit women to priestly ordination. The Sacred Congregation deems it opportune at the present juncture to explain this position of the Church. It is a position which will perhaps cause pain but whose positive value will become apparent in the long run, since it can be of help in deepening understanding of the respective roles of men and of women.

1. *The Church's constant tradition*
The Catholic Church has never felt that priestly or episcopal ordination can be validly conferred on women. A few heretical sects in the first centuries, especially Gnostic ones, entrusted the exercise of the priestly ministry to women: this innovation was immediately noted and condemned by the Fathers, who considered it as unacceptable in the Church.[7] It is true that in the writings of the Fathers one will find the undeniable influence of prejudices unfavourable to women, but nevertheless, it should be noted that these prejudices had hardly any influence on their pastoral activity, and still less on their spiritual direction. But over and above considerations inspired by the spirit of the times, one finds expressed – especially in the canonical documents of the Antiochian and Egyptian – this

essential reason, namely, that by calling only men to the priestly Order and ministry in its true sense, the Church intends to remain faithful to the type of ordained ministry willed by the Lord Jesus Christ and carefully maintained by the Apostles.[8]

The same conviction animates mediaeval theology,[9] even if the Scholastic doctors, in their desire to clarify by reason the data of faith, often present arguments on this point that modern thought would have difficulty in admitting or would even rightly reject. Since that period and up to our own time, it can be said that the question has not been raised again, for the practice has enjoyed peaceful and universal acceptance.

The Church's tradition in the matter has thus been so firm in the course of the centuries that the Magisterium has not felt the need to intervene in order to formulate a principle which was not attacked, or to defend a law which was not challenged. But each time that this tradition had the occasion to manifest itself, it witnessed to the Church's desire to conform to the model left to her by the Lord.

The same tradition has been faithfully safeguarded by the Churches of the East. Their unanimity on this point is all the more remarkable since in many other questions their discipline admits of a great diversity. At the present time these same Churches refuse to associate themselves with requests directed towards securing the accession of women to priestly ordination.

2. *The attitude of Christ*

Jesus Christ did not call any woman to become part of the Twelve. If he acted in this way, it was not in order to conform to the customs of his time, for his attitude towards women was quite different from that of his milieu, and he deliberately and courageously broke with it.

For example, to the great astonishment of his own

disciples Jesus converses publicly with the Samaritan woman (cf. Jn 4:27); he takes no notice of the state of legal impurity of the woman who had suffered from haemorrhages (cf. Mt 9:20-22); he allows a sinful woman to approach him in the house of Simon the Pharisee (cf. Lk 7:37ff.); and by pardoning the woman taken in adultery, he means to show that one must not be more severe towards the fault of a woman than towards that of a man (cf. Jn 8:11). He does not hesitate to depart from the Mosaic Law in order to affirm the equality of the rights and duties of men and women with regard to the marriage bond (cf.Mk 10:2-11; Mt 19:3-9).

In his itinerant ministry Jesus was accompanied not only by the Twelve but also by a group of women: "Mary, surnamed the Magdalene, from whom seven demons had gone out, Joanna the wife of Herod's steward Chuza, Susanna, and several others who provided for them out of their own resources"(Lk 8:2-3). Contrary to the Jewish mentality, which did not accord great value to the testimony of women, as Jewish law attests, it was nevertheless women who were the first to have the privilege of seeing the risen Lord, and it was they who were charged by Jesus to take the first paschal message to the Apostles themselves (cf. Mt 28:7-10; Lk 24:9-10, Jn 20:11-18), in order to prepare the latter to become the official witnesses to the Resurrection.

It is true that these facts do not make the matter immediately obvious. This is no surprise, for the questions that the Word of God brings before us go beyond the obvious. In order to reach the ultimate meaning of the mission of Jesus and the ultimate meaning of Scripture, a purely historical exegesis of the texts cannot suffice. But it must be recognized that we have here a number of convergent indications that make all the more remarkable the fact that Jesus did not entrust the apostolic charge[10] to women. Even his Mother, who was so closely associated with the mystery of her Son, and whose incomparable role is emphasized by the Gospels of Luke and John, was not in vested with the apostolic ministry. This fact was to lead the Fathers to present her as the example of Christ's will in this domain; as Pope Innocent III repeated later, at the beginning of the thirteenth century, "Although the Blessed Virgin Mary surpassed in dignity and in excellence all the Apostles, nevertheless it was not to her but to them that the Lord entrusted the keys of the Kingdom of Heaven".[11]

3. The practice of the apostles

The apostolic community remained faithful to the attitude of Jesus towards women. Although Mary occupied a privileged place in the little circle of those gathered in the Upper Room after the Lord's Ascension (cf. Acts 1:14), it was not she who was called to enter the College of the Twelve at the time of the election that resulted in the choice of Matthias: those who were put forward were two disciples whom the Gospels do not even mention.

On the day of Penteconst, the Holy Spirit filled them all, men and women (cf. Acts 2:1; 1:14), yet the proclamation of the fulfilment of the prophecies in Jesus was made only by "Peter and the Eleven" (Acts 2:14).

When they and Paul went beyond the confines of the Jewish world, the preaching of the Gospel and the Christian life in the Greco-Roman civilization impelled them to break with Mosaic practices, sometimes regretfully. They could therefore have envisaged conferring ordination on women, if they had not been convinced of their duty of fidelity to the Lord on this point. In the Hellenistic world, the cult of a number of pagan divinities was entrusted to priestesses. In fact the Greeks did not share the ideas of the Jews: although their philosophers taught the inferiority of women, historians nevertheless emphasize the existence of a certain movement for the advancement of women during the Imperial period. In fact we know from the book of the Acts and from the Letters of Saint Paul that certain women worked with the Apostle for the Gospel (cf. Rom 16:3-12; Phil 4:3). Saint Paul lists their names with gratitude in the final salutions of the Letters. Some of them often exercised an important influence of conversions: Priscilla, Lydia and others; especially Priscilla, who took it on herself to complete the instruction of Apollos (cf. Acts 18:26); Phoebe, in the service of the Church of Cenchreae (cf. Rom. 16:1). All these facts manifest within the Apostolic Church a considerable evolution vis-a-vis the customs of Judaism. Nevertheless at no time was there a question of conferring ordination on these women.

In the Pauline Letters, exegetes of authority have noted a difference between two formulas used by the Apostle: he writes indiscriminately "my fellow workers" (Rom 16:3; Phil 4:2-3) when referring to men and women helping him in his apostolate in one way or another; but he reserves the title "God's fellow workers" (1 Cor 3:9; cf. 1 Thess 3:2) to Apollos, Timothy and himself, thus designated because they are directly set apart for the apostolic ministry and the preaching of the Word of God. In spite of the so important role played by women on the day of the Resurrection, their collaboration was not extended by Saint Paul to the official and public proclamation of the message, since this proclamation belongs exclusively to the apostolic mission.

4. *Permanent value of the attitude of Jesus and the Apostles*

Could the Church today depart from this attitude of

Jesus and the Apostles, which has been considered as
normative by the whole of tradition up to our own day?
Various arguments have been put forward in favour of a
positive reply to this question, and these must now be
examined.

It has been claimed in particular that the attitude of
Jesus and the Apostles is explained by the influence of
their millieu and their times. It is said that, if Jesus did
not entrust to women and not even to his Mother a
ministry assimilating them to the Twelve, this was
because historical circumstances did not permit him to
do so. No one however has ever proved - and it is
clearly impossible to prove - that this attitude is inspired
only by social and cultural reasons. As we have seen, an
examination of the Gospels shows on the contrary that
Jesus broke with the prejudices of his time, by widely
contravening the discriminations practised with regard
to women. One therefore cannot maintain that, by not
calling women to enter the group of the Apostles, Jesus
was simply letting himself be guided by reasons of
expediency. For all the more reason, social and cultural
conditioning did not hold back the Apostles working in
the Greek millieu, where the same forms of discrimination did not exist.

Another objection is based upon the transitory
character that one claims to see today in some of the
prescriptions of Saint Paul concerning women, and
upon the difficulties that some aspects of his teaching
raise in this regard. But it must be noted that these
ordinances, probably inspired by the customs of the
period, concern scarcely more than disciplinary practices of minor importance, such as the obligation
imposed upon women to wear a veil on the head (1 Cor
11:2-6); such requirements no longer have a normative
value. However, the Apostle's forbidding of women
"to speak" in the assemblies (cf. 1 Cor 14:34-35; 1 Tim
2:12) is of a different nature, and exegetes define its

meaning in this way: Paul in no way opposes the right, which he elsewhere recognizes as possessed by women to prophesy in the assembly (cf. 1 Cor 11:5); the prohibition solely concerns the official function of teaching in the Christian assembly. For Saint Paul this prescription is bound up with the divine plan of creation (cf. 1 Cor 11:7, Gen 2:18-24); it would be difficult to see in it the expression of a cultural fact. Nor should it be forgotten that we owe to Saint Paul one of the most vigorous texts in the New Testament on the fundamental equality of men and women, as children of God in Christ (cf. Gal. 3:28). Therefore there is no reason for accusing him of prejudices against women, when we note the trust that he shows towards them and the collaboration that he asks of them in his apostolate.

But over and above these objections taken from the history of apostolic times, those who support the legitimacy of change in the matter turn to the Church's practice in her sacramental discipline. It has been noted in our day especially, to what extent the Church is conscious of possessing a certain power over the sacraments, even though they were instituted by Christ. She has used this power down the centuries in order to determine their signs and the conditions of their administration: recent decisions of Popes Pius XII and Paul VI are proof of this.[12] However, it must be emphasized that this power, which is a real one, has definite limits. As Pope Pius XII recalled: " The Church has no power over the substance of the sacraments, that is to say, over what Christ the Lord, as the sources of Revelation bear witness, determined should be maintained in the sacramental sign".[13] This was already the teaching of the Council of Trent, which declared: "In the Church there has always existed this power, that in the administration of the sacraments, provided that their substance remains unaltered, she can lay down or modify what she considers more fitting either for the benefit of those who receive them or for respect towards those same sacraments, according to varying circumstances, times or places".[14]

Moreover, it must not be forgotten that the sacramental signs are not conventional ones. Not only is it true that, in many respects, they are natural signs because they respond to the deep symbolism of actions and things, but they are more than this: they are principally meant to link the person of every period to the supreme Event of the history of salvation, in order to enable that person to understand, through all the Bible's wealth of pedagogy and symbolism, what grace they signify and produce. For example, the sacrament of the Eucharist is not only a fraternal meal, but at the same time the memorial which makes present and actual Christ's sacrifice and his offering by the Church. Again, the priestly ministry is not just a pastoral service; it ensures the continuity of the functions entrusted by Christ to the Apostles and the continuity of the powers related to those functions. Adaptation to civilizations and times therefore cannot abolish, on essential points, the sacramental reference to constitutive events of Christianity and to Christ himself.

In the final analysis it is the Church, through the voice of her Magisterium, that, in these various domains, decides what can change and what must remain immutable. When she judges that she cannot accept certain changes, it is because she knows that she is bound by Christ's manner of acting. Her attitude, despite appearances, is therefore not one of archaism but of fidelity: it can be truly understood only in this light. The Church makes pronouncements in virtue of the Lord's promise and the presence of the Holy Spirit, in order to proclaim better the mystery of Christ and to safeguard and manifest the whole of its rich content.

This practice of the Church therefore has a normative character: in the fact of conferring priestly ordination only on men, it is a question of an unbroken tradition throughout the history of the Church, universal in the East and in the West, and alert to repress abuses immediately. This norm, based on Christ's example, has been and is still observed because it is considered to conform to God's plan for his Church.

5. *The ministerial Priesthood in the light of the mystery of Christ*

Having recalled the Church's norm and the basis thereof, it seems useful and opportune to illustrate this norm by showing the profound fittingness that theological reflection discovers between the proper nature of the sacrament of Order, with its specific reference to the mystery of Christ, and the fact that only men have been called to receive priestly ordination. It is not a question here of bringing forward a demonstrative argument, but of clarifying this teaching by the analogy of faith.

The Church's constant teaching, repeated and clarified by the Second Vatican Council and again recalled by the 1971 Synod of Bishops and by the Sacred Congregation for the Doctrine of the Faith in its Declaration of 24 June 1973, declares that the bishop or the priest, in the exercise of his ministry, does not act in his own name, *in persona propria:* he represents Christ, who acts through him: "the priest truly acts in the place of Christ", as Saint Cyprian already wrote in the third century.[15] It is this ability to represent Christ that Saint Paul considered as characteristic of his apostolic function (cf. 2 Cor 5: 20; Gal 4:14). The supreme expression of this representation is found in the altogether special form it assumes in the celebration of the Eucharist, which is the source and centre of the Church's unity, the sacrificial meal in which the People of God are associated in the sacrifice of Christ; the priest, who alone has the power to perform it, then acts not only through the effective power conferred on him by

Christ, but *in persona Christi*,[16] taking the role of Christ, to the point of being his very image, when he pronounces the words of consecration.[17]

The Christian priesthood is therefore of a sacramental nature: the priest is a sign, the supernatural effectiveness of which comes from the ordination received, but a sign that must be perceptible[18] and which the faithful must be able to recognize with ease. The whole sacramental economy is in fact based upon natural signs, on symbols imprinted upon the human psychology: "Sacramental signs", says Saint Thomas, "represent what they signify by natural resemblance".[19] The same natural resemblance is required for persons as for things: when Christ's role in the Eucharist is to be expressed sacramentally, there would not be this "natural resemblance" which must exist betwen Christ and his minister if the role of Christ were not taken by a man: in such a case it would be difficult to see in the minister the image of Christ. For Christ himself was and remains a man.

Christ is of course the firstborn of all humanity, of women as well as men: the unity which he re-established after sin is such that there are no more distinctions between Jew and Greek, slave and free, male and female, but all are one in Christ Jesus (cf. Gal 3:28). Nevertheless, the Incarnation of the Word took place according to the male sex: this is indeed a question of fact, and this fact, while not implying an alleged natural superiority of man over woman, cannot be disassociated from the economy of salvation: it is, indeed, in harmony with the entirety of God's plan as God himself has revealed it, and of which the mystery of the Covenant is the nucleus.

For the salvation offered by God to men and women, the union with him to which they are called – in short, the Covenant – took on, from the Old Testament Prophets onwards, the privileged form of a nuptial mystery: for God the Chosen People is seen as his ardently loved spouse. Both Jewish and Christian tradition has discovered the depth of this intimacy of love by reading and rereading the Song of Songs; the divine Bridegroom will remain faithful even when the Bride betrays his love, when Israel is unfaithful to God (cf. Hos 1-3; Jer 2). When the "fullness of time" (Gal 4:4) comes, the Word, the Son of God, takes on flesh in order to establish and seal the new and eternal Covenant in his blood, which will be shed for many so that sins may be forgiven. His death will gather together again the scattered children of God; from his pierced side will be born the Church, as Eve was born from Adam's side. At that time there is fully and eternally accomplished the nuptial mystery proclaimed and hymned in the Old Testament: Christ is the Bridegroom; the Church is his bride, whom he loves because he has gained her by his blood and made her glorious, holy and without blemish, and henceforth he is inseparable from her. This nuptial theme, which is developed from the Letters of Saint Paul onwards (cf. 2 Cor 11:2; Eph 5:22-23) to the writings of Saint John (cf. especially Jn 3:29; Rev 19:7,9), is present also in the Synoptic Gospels: the Bridegroom's friend must not fast as long as he is with them (cf. Mk 2:19); the Kingdom of heaven is like a king who gave a feast for his son's wedding (cf. Mt 22:1-14). It is through this Scriptural language, all interwoven with symbols, and which expresses and affects man and woman in their profound identity, that there is revealed to us the mystery of God and Christ, a mystery which of itself is unfathomable.

That is why we can never ignore the fact that Christ is a man. And therefore, unless one is to disregard the importance of this symbolism for the economy of Revelation, it must be admitted that, in actions which demand the character of ordination and in which Christ himself, the author of the Covenant, the Bridegroom and Head of the Church, is represented, exercising his ministry of salvation – which is in the highest degree the case of the Eucharist – his role (this is the original sense of the word *persona*) must be taken by a man. This does not stem from any personal superiority of the latter in the order of values, but only from a difference of fact on the level of functions and service.

Could one say that, since Christ is now in the heavenly condition, from now on it is a matter of indifference whether he be represented by a man or by a woman, since "at the resurrection men and women do not marry" (Mt 22:30)? But this text does not mean that the distinction between man and woman, insofar as it determines the identity proper to the person, is suppressed in the glorified state; what holds for us holds also for Christ. It is indeed evident that in human beings the difference of sex exercises an important influence, much deeper than, for example ethnic differences: the latter do not affect the human person as intimately as the difference of sex, which is directly ordained both for the communion of persons and for the generation of human beings. In Biblical Revelation this difference is the effect of God's will from the beginning: "male and female he created them"(Gen 1:27).

However, it will perhaps be further objected that the priest, especially when he presides at the liturgical and sacramental functions, equally represents the Church: he acts in her name with "the intention of doing what she does". In this sense, the theologians of the Middle Ages said that the minister also acts *in persona Ecclesiae*, that is to say, in the name of the whole Church and in order to represent her. And in fact, leaving aside the question of the participation of the faithful in a liturgical action, it is indeed in the name of the whole Church that the action is celebrated by the priest: he prays in the name of all, and in the Mass he offers the sacrifice of the whole Church. In the new Passover, the Church, under visible signs, immolates Christ through the ministry of the priest.[20] And so, it is asserted, since the priest also represents the Church, would it not be possible to think that this representation could be carried out by a woman, according to the symbolism already explained? It is true that the priest represents the Church, which is the Body of Christ. But if he does so, it is precisely because he first represents Christ himself, who is the Head and Shepherd of the Church. The Second Vatican Council[21] used this phrase to make more precise and to complete the expression *in persona Christi*. It is in this quality that the priest presides over the Christian assembly and celebrates the Eucharistic sacrifice "in which the whole Church offers and is herself wholly offered".[22]

If one does justice to these reflections, one will better understand how well-founded is the basis of the Church's practice; and one will conclude that the controversies raised in our days over the ordination of women are for all Christians pressing invitation to meditate on the mystery of the Church, to study in greater detail the meaning of the episcopate and the priesthood, and to rediscover the real and pre-eminent place of the priest in the community of the baptized, of which he indeed forms part but from which he is distinguished because, in the action that call for the character of ordination, for the community he is – with all the effectiveness proper to the sacraments – the image and symbol of Christ himself who calls, forgives, and accomplishes the sacrifice of the Covenant.

6. *The ministerial Priesthood illustrated by the mystery of the Church*

It is opportune to recall that problems of sacramental theology, especially when they concern the ministerial priesthood, as is the case here, cannot be solved except in the light of Revelation. The human sciences, however valuable their contribution in their own domain, cannot suffice here, for they cannot grasp the realities of faith: the properly supernatural content of these realities is beyond their competence.

Thus one must note the extent to which the Church is a society different from other societies, original in her nature and in her structures. The pastoral charge in the Church is normally linked to the sacrament of Order: it is not a simple government, comparable to the modes of authority found in States. It is not granted by people's spontaneous choice: even when it involves designation through election, it is the laying on of hands and the prayer of the successors of the Apostles which guarantee God's choice; and it is the Holy Spirit, given by ordination, who grants participation in the ruling power of the Supreme Pastor, Christ (cf. Acts 20:28). It is a charge of service and love: "If you love me, feed my sheep" (cf. Jn 21:15-17).

For this reason one cannot see how it is possible to propose the admission of women to the priesthood in virtue of the equality of right of the human person, an equality which holds good also for Christians. To this end use is sometimes made of the text quoted above, from the Letter to the Galatians (3:28), which says that in Christ there is no longer any distinction between men and women. But this passage does not concern ministries: it only affirms the universal calling to divine filiation, which is the same for all. Moreover, and above all, to consider the ministerial priesthood as a human right would be to misjudge its nature completely: baptism does not confer any personal title to public ministry in the Church. The priesthood is not conferred for the honour or advantage of the recipient, but for the service of God and the Church; it is the object of a specific and totally gratuitous vocation: "You did not choose me, no, I chose you; and I commissioned you . .' (Jn 15:16; cf. Heb 5:4).

It is sometimes said and written in books and

periodicals that some women feel that they have a vocation to the priesthood. Such an attraction, however noble and understandable, still does not suffice for a genuine vocation. In fact a vocation cannot be reduced to a mere personal attraction, which can remain purely subjective. Since the priesthood is a particular ministry of which the Church has received the charge and the control, authentication by the Church is indispensable here and is a constitutive part of the vocation: Christ chose "those he wanted" (Mk 3:13). On the other hand, there is a universal vocation of all the baptized to the exercise of the royal priesthood by offering their lives to God and by giving witness for his praise.

Women who express a desire for the ministerial priesthood are doubtless motivated by the desire to serve Christ and the Church. And it is not surprising that, at a time when they are becoming more aware of the discriminations to which they have been subject, they should desire the ministerial priesthood itself. But it must not be forgotten that the priesthood does not form part of the rights of the individual, but stems from the economy of the mystery of Christ and the Church. The priestly office cannot become the goal of social advancement; no merely human progress of society or of the individual can of itself give access to it: it is of another order.

It therefore remains for us to meditate more deeply on the nature of the real equality of the baptized which is one of the great affirmations of Christianity: equality is in no way identity, for the Church is a differentiated body, in which each individual has his or her role. The roles are distinct, and must not be confused; they do not favour the superiority of some vis-á-vis the others, nor do they provide an excuse for jealousy; the only better gift, which can and must be desired, is love (cf. 1Cor 12-13). The greatest in the Kingdom of Heaven are not the ministers but the saints.

The Church desires that Christian women should become fully aware of the greatness of their mission; today their role is of capital importance, both for the renewal and humanization of society and for the rediscovery by believers of the true face of the Church.

Notes

1. AAS 55 (1963), pp. 267-268.
2. Cf. Second Vatican Council, Pastoral Constitution *Gaudium et Spes*. 29 (7 December 1965); AAS 58 (1966), pp. 1048-1049.
3. Cf. Pope Paul VI, Address to the members of the Study Commission on the Role ofWomen in Society and in the Church and to the members of the Committee for International Women's Year, 18 April 1975: AAS 67 (1975), p. 265.
4. Second Vatican Council, Decree *Apostolican Actuositatem*, 9 (18 November 1965): AAS 58 (1966), p. 846.
5. Cf. Pope Paul VI, Address to the members of the Study Commission on the Role of Women in Society and in the Church and to the members of the Committee for International Women's Year, 18 April 1975: AAS 67 (1975), p. 266.
6. Cf. AAS 68 (1976), pp. 599-600; cf. *Ibid.*, pp. 600-601.
7. Saint Irenacus, *Adversus Haereses*, 1, 13, 2: PG 7, 580-581; ed. Harvey, I, 114-122; Tertullian, *De Praescrip, Haeretic*, 41, 5: CCL 1, p. 221; Firmilian of Caesarea, in Saint Cyprian, *Epist.*, 75; CSEL 3, pp. 817-818; Origen, *Fragmentum in I Cor.* 74, in *Journal of Theological Studies* 10 (1909), pp. 41-42; Saint Epiphanius, *Panarion* 49, 2-3; 78, 23; 79, 2-4; vol. 2, GCS 31, pp. 243-244; vol. 3, GCS 37, pp. 473, 477-479.
8. *Didascalia Apostolorum*, ch. 15, ed. R.H. Connolly, pp. 133 and 142; *Constitutiones Apostolicae, bk. 3, ch. 6, nos. 1-2; ch. 9, 3-4; ed. F.H. Funk, pp. 191; 201; Saint John Chrysostom, De Sacerdotio* 2, 2: PH 48, 633.
9. Saint Bonaventure, *In IV Sent.*, Dist. 25, art. 2, q. 1, ed. Quaracchi, vol. 4, 649; Richard of Middleton, *In IV Sent.*, Dist. 25, art. 4, n. 1, ed. Venice, 1499, f° 177r; John Duns Scotus, *In IV Sent., Dist.* 25: *Opus Oxoniense*, ed. Vives, vol. 19, p. 140; *Reportata Parisiensia*, vol. 24, pp. 369-371; Durandus of Saint-Pourcain, *In IV Sent.*, Dist. 25, q. 2, ed. Venice, 1571, f° 364v.
10. Some who also wished to explain this fact by a symbolic intention of Jesus: the Twelve were to represent the ancestors of the twelve tribes of Israel (cf. *Mt* 19-28; *Lk* 22:30). But in these texts it is only a question of their participation in the eschatological judgment. The essential meaning of the choice of the Twelve should rather be sought in the totality of their mission (cf. *Mk* 3:14): they are to represent Jesus to the people and carry on his work.

11. Pope Innocent III, *Epist.* (11 December 1210) to the Bishops of Palencia and Burgos, included in *Corpus Iuris, Decret. Lib. 5*, tit. 38, *De Paenit.*, ch. 10 *Nova:* ed. , Friedberg, vol. 2, col. 886-887; cf. *Glossa in Decretal. Lib. I*, tit. 33, ch. 12 *Dilecta, v Iurisdictioni.* Cf. Saint Thomas, *Summa Theologiae*, III, q. 27, a. 5 ad 3; Pseudo-Albert the Great, *Mariale*, quaest. 42, ed. Borgnet 37, 81.

12. Pope Pius XII, Apostolic Constitution *Sacramentum Ordinis, 30 November 1947: AAS 40 (1948)*, pp. 5-7; Pope Paul VI, *Apostolic Constitution Divinae Consortium Naturae*, 15 August 1971: AAS 63, (1971), pp. 657-664; Apostolic Constitution *Sacram Unctionem*, 30 November 1972: AAS 65 (1973), pp. 5-9.

13. Pope Pius XII, Apostolic Constitution *Sacramentum Ordinis: loc. cit.*, p. 5.

14. Session 21, chap. 2: Denzinger-Schonmetzer, *Enchiridion Symbolorum* 1728.

15. Saint Cyprian, *Epist.* 63, 14: PL 4, 397 B; ed. Hartel, vol. 3, p. 713.

16. Second Vatican Council, Constitution *Sacrosanctum Concilium*, 33 (4 December 1963): " . . . by the priest who presides over the assembly in the person of Christ . . . "; Dogmatic Constitution *Lumen Gentium*, 10 (21 November 1964): "The ministerial priest, by the sacred power he enjoys, moulds and rules the priestly people. Acting in the person of Christ, he brings about the Eucharistic Sacrifice, and offers it to God in the name of all the people . . " 28: "By the powers of the sacrament of Order, and in the image of Christ the eternal High Priest . . they exercise this sacred function of Christ above all in the Eucharistic liturgy or synaxis. There, acting in the person of Christ . . ": Decree *Presbyterorum Ordinis*, 2 (7 December, 1965): " . . . priests, by the anointing of the Holy Spirit, are marked with a special character and are so configured to Christ the Priest that they can act in the person of Christ the Head"; 13: "As ministers of sacred realities, especially in the Sacrifice of the Mass, priests represent the person of Christ in a special way"; cf. 1971 Synod of Bishops, *De Sacerdotio Ministeriali* I, 4; Sacred Congregation for the Doctrine of the Faith, *Declaratio circa catholicam doctrinam de Ecclesia*, 6 (24 June 1973).

17. Saint Thomas, *Summa Theologiae*, III, q. 83, art. 1, ad 3: "It is to be said that (just as the celebration of this sacrament is the representative image of Christ's Cross: *ibid.* ad 2), for the same reason the priest also enacts the image of Christ, in whose person and by whose power he pronounces the words of consecration".

18. "For since a sacrament is a sign, there is required in the things that are done in the sacraments not only the 'res' by the signification of the 'res'", recalls Saint Thomas, precisely in order to reject the ordination of women: *In IV Sent.*, dist. 25, q. 2, art. 1, quaestiuncula 1a, corp.

19. Saint Thomas, *In IV Sent.*, dist. 25, q. 2, quaestiuncula 1a ad 4um.

20 Cf. Council of Trent, Session 22, chap. 1: DS 1741.

21. Second Vatican Council, Dogmatic Counstitution *Lumen Gentium*, 28: "Exercising within the limits of their authority the function of Christ as Shepherd and Head"; Decree *Presbyterorum Ordinis* 2: "that they can act

in the person of Christ the Head"; 6: "the office of Christ the Head and the Shepherd". Cf. Pope Pius XII, Encyclical Letter *Mediator Dei:* "the minister of the altar represents the person of Christ as the Head, offering in the name of all his members": AAS 39 (1947), p. 556; 1971 Synod of Bishops, *De Sacerdotio Ministeriali,* I, 4: "(The priestly ministry) . . . makes Christ, the Head of the community, present . . .".

22. Pope Paul VI, Encyclical Letter *Mysterium Fidei,* 3 September 1965: AAS 57 (1965), p. 761.

Anglican-Orthodox Joint Doctrinal Commission, Athens July 1978

The Orthodox position on the Ordination of Women to the Priesthood

The Orthodox members of the Commission unanimously affirm the following:

(1) God created mankind in his image as male and female, establishing a diversity of functions and gifts. These functions are complementary but, as St Paul insists (1 Cor. 12), not all are interchangeable. In the life of the Church, as in that of the family, God has assigned certain tasks and forms of ministry specifically to the man, and others – different, yet no less important – to the woman. There is every reason for Christians to oppose current trends which make men and women interchangeable in their functions and roles, and thus lead to the dehumanization of life.

(2) The Orthodox Church honours a woman, the Holy Virgin Mary, the Theotokos, as the human person closest to God. In the Orthodox tradition women saints are given such titles as *megalomartys* (great martyr) and *isapostolos* (equal to the apostles). Thus it is clear that in no sense does the Orthodox Church consider women to be intrinsically inferior in God's eyes. Men and women are equal but different, and we need to recognize this diversity of gifts. Both in discussion among themselves and in dialogue with other Christians the Orthodox recognize the duty of the Church to give women more opportunities to use their specific *charismata* (gifts) for

the benefit of the whole people of God. Among the ministries (*diakoniai*) exercised by women in the Church we note the following:

(i) ministries of a diaconal and philanthropic kind, involving the pastoral care of the sick and needy, of refugees and many others, and issuing in various forms of social responsibility,

(ii) ministries of prayer and intercession, of spiritual help and guidance, particularly but not exclusively in connection with the monastic communities,

(iii) ministries connected with teaching and instruction, particularly in the field of the Church's missionary activity,

(iv) ministries connected with the administration of the Church.

This list is not meant to be exhaustive. It indicates some of the areas where we believe that women and men are called to work together in the service of God's Kingdom, and where the many *charismata* of the Holy Spirit may function freely and fruitfully in the building up of the Church and society.

(3) But, while women exercise this diversity of ministries, it is not possible for them to be admitted to the priesthood. The ordination of women to the priesthood is an innovation, lacking any basis whatever in Holy Tradition. The Orthodox Church takes very seriously the admonition of St Paul, where the Apostle states with emphasis, repeating himself twice: 'But if we or an angel from heaven, preaches to you anything else than what we have preached to you, let him be anathema. As we have already said, so I say to you now once more: if anyone preaches to you anything else than what you have received, let him be anathema' (Gal. 1.8-9).

From the time of Christ and the apostles onwards, the Church has ordained only men to the priesthood. Christians today are bound to remain faithful to the example of our Lord, to the testimony of Scripture, and to the constant and unvarying practice of the Church for two thousand years. In this constant and unvarying practice we see revealed the will of God and the testimony of the Holy Spirit, and we know that the Holy Spirit does not contradict himself.

(4) Holy Tradition is not static, but living and creative. Tradition is received by each succeeding generation in the same way, but in its own situation, and thus it is verified and enriched by the renewed experience that the People of God are continually gaining. On the basis of this renewed experience, the Spirit teaches us to be always responsive to the needs of the contemporary world. The Spirit does not bring us a new revelation, but enables us to relive the truth revealed once for all in Jesus Christ, and continuously present in the Church. It is important, therefore, to distinguish between innovations and the creative continuity of Tradition. We Orthodox see the ordination of women, not as part of this creative continuity, but as a violation of the apostolic faith and order of the Church.

(5) The action of ordaining women to the priesthood involves not simply a canonical point of Church discipline, but the basis of the Christian faith as expressed in the Church's ministries. If the Anglicans continue to ordain women to the priesthood, this will have a decisively negative effect on the issue of the recognition of Anglican Orders. Those Orthodox Churches which have partially or provisionally recognized Anglican Orders did so on the ground that the Anglican Church has preserved the apostolic succession; and the apostolic succession is not merely continuity in the outward laying on of hands, but signifies continuity in apostolic faith and spiritual life. By ordaining women, Anglicans would sever themselves from this continuity, and so any existing acts of recognition by the Orthodox would have to be reconsidered.

IV Anglican Positions on the Ordination of Women to the Priesthood

(1) The Anglican members of the Commission are unanimous in their desire to accept and maintain the tradition of the gospel, to which the prophets and apostles bear witness, and to be true to it in the life of the Church. They are divided over the ways in which that tradition should respond to the pressures of the world, over the extent to which the tradition may develop and change, and over the criteria by which to determine what developments within it are legitimate and appropriate. In the case of the ordination of women differences have become particularly acute and divisive within the Anglican Communion, now that the convictions of those in favour of it have been translated into action in certain national churches.

(2) On this question there is a diversity of views in the Anglican Communion and among the members of the Commission. There are those who believe that the ordination of women to the priesthood and the episcopate is in no way consonant with a true understanding of the Church's catholicity and apostolocity, but rather constitutes a grave deformation of the Church's traditional faith and order. They therefore hope that under the guidance of the Holy Spirit, this practice will come to cease in our churches.

There are others who believe that the actions already taken constitute a proper extension and development of the Church's traditional ministry, and a necessary and prophetic response to the changing circumstances in which some churches are placed. They hope that in due time, under the guidance of the Spirit, these actions will be universally accepted.

There are others who regret the way in which the present action has been taken and believe that the time was not opportune nor the method appropriate for such action, although they see no absolute objection to it. Some of them hope that a way forward may be found which will allow for the distinct and complementary contributions of men and women to the Church's ordained ministry.

The minutes of the 1978 Athens Conference add the following presentation of Anglican views which were expressed at the time:

(1) Those Anglicans who in principle oppose the ordination of women do so for the reasons advanced by the Orthodox in this report. They would express their reasons as follows: the claim of the Anglican Communion to be catholic means that compelling reasons must be demonstrated for the rightness of such a break with catholic tradition. Those who oppose such a break believe that such reasons have not been forthcoming. On the contrary, they believe that there are fundamental reasons why such a break should not be made. These, in their judgement, come from a consideration of the Person of Christ. Although there is neither maleness nor femaleness in God, it was in a male that the Word was made flesh and humanity in all its fullness was united to the Godhead. They believe that this fact expresses the truth that the initiative in our redemption lies wholly with God, to whom the response of humanity must be creative obedience. For a women to be the icon or sacramental expression of Christ as Head of the Church seems to them to be in opposition to the biblical images of the Church in relation to God, which consistently stress that humanity and the Church must be feminine in relation to God.

The New Testament indicates that the issue of headship and authority, however qualified, cannot be divorced either from the created relationship between man and woman, for instance in marriage, or from the instituted relationship between the ordained ministry and the congregation. They believe that a male priest must be the symbol and image of Christ as Bridegroom, whereas women, supremely exemplified in Mary, to whom was given the highest vocation of any created being, must be the symbol and image of the response of humanity in creative obedience. They believe that the God-given nature of the ministerial priesthood includes the fact that it is male. A refusal to accept this fact leads in their judgement, not only to a distortion of man's understanding of his relationship to God, but also to a distortion of his understanding of the redemption of the deepest aspects of his humanity. Finally, the opponents believe that the ordination of women to the priesthood is divisive because it is wrong, rather than wrong because it is divisive.

(2) Those members of the Commission who advocate the ordination of women to the priesthood now, do so because they believe that the Church's tradition must grow and develop if the Church is to remain faithful to its mission to the world. More particularly, they believe that this is a true development, under the guidance of the Holy Spirit, of the patterns of ministry to which God has been calling some Churches in response to major changes in the ordering of society. The vocations of women who offer themselves for the priestly ministry require therefore to be tested, and none of the arguments, either from Scripture or tradition, advanced against such vocations seem to those who hold this position to be in principle convincing. In particular they hold that arguments which suggest that priests must be male in order either to represent the maleness of God, a position held by no one in this Commission, or because the maleness of Christ is of soteriological significance, are based on serious doctrinal errors. Since priesthood represents humanity to God and God to humanity, it is

humanity and not maleness which is the decisive qualification for exercising priesthood, just as in Christ, according to catholic doctrine, it is his humanity which is of soteriological significance and not the accidents of his humanity. Further they argue that to insist on an all-male priesthood in societies which have abandoned all-male leadership in other areas of life is in effect to distort the meaning of Christian priesthood. This may lead to serious distortions in doctrine. Thirdly, they believe that the ordination of women would lead to an enrichment of the Christian priesthood by bringing to it women's gifts and wisdom, as well as by deepening the Christian understanding of the divine saving initiative in Jesus Christ which is represented by the priesthood.

(3) There are other members of the Commission who, while they find these theological arguments valid and convincing, yet believe for reasons of an ecclesiological nature that action in this matter should not be taken precipitately.

English language version Copyright c Henry Hill and Methodios of Thyateira and Great Britain 1985

Baptism, Eucharist and Ministry

Faith and Order Paper III (1982)

Ordained Ministry and Authority

15. The authority of the ordained minister is rooted in Jesus Christ, who has received it from the Father (Matt. 28:18), and who confers it by the Holy Spirit through the act of ordination. This act takes place within a community which accords public recognition to a particular person. Because Jesus came as one who serves (Mark 10:45; Luke 22:27), to be set apart means to be consecrated to service. Since ordination is essentially a setting apart with prayer for the gift of the Holy Spirit, the authority of the ordained ministry is not to be understood as the possession of the ordained person but as a gift for the continuing edification of the body in and for which the minister has been ordained. Authority has the character of responsibility before God and is exercised with the cooperation of the whole community.

16. Therefore, ordained ministers must not be autocrats or impersonal functionaries. Although called to exercise wise and loving leadership on the basis of the Word of God, they are bound to the faithful in inter-dependence and reciprocity. Only when they seek the response and acknowledgement of the community can their authority be protected from the distortions of isolation and domination. They manifest and exercise the authority of Christ in the way Christ himself revealed God's

authority to the world, by committing their life to the community. Christ's authority is unique. "He spoke as one who has authority (*exousia*), not as the scribes" (Matt. 7:29). This authority is an authority governed by love for the "sheep who have no shepherd" (Matt. 9:36). It is confirmed by his life of service and, supremely, by his death and resurrection. Authority in the Church can only be authentic as it seeks to conform to this model.

C. Ordained Ministry and Priesthood

17. Jesus Christ is the unique priest of the new covenant. Christ's life was given as a sacrifice for all. Derivatively, the Church as a whole can be described as a priesthood. All members are called to offer their being "as a living sacrifice" and to intercede for the Church and the salvation of the world. Ordained ministers are related, as are all Christians, both to the priesthood of Christ, and to the priesthood of the Church. But they may appropriately be called priests because they fulfil a particular priestly service by strengthening and building up the royal and prophetic priesthood of the faithful through word and sacraments, through their prayers of intercession, and through their pastoral guidance of the community.

D. The Ministry of Men and Women in the Church

18. Where Christ is present, human barriers are being broken. The Church is called to convey to the world the image of a new humanity. There is in Christ no male or female (Gal. 3:28). Both women and men must discover together their contributions to the service of Christ in the Church. The Church must discover the ministry which can be provided by women as well as that which can be provided by men. A deeper understanding of the comprehensiveness of ministry which reflects the interdependence of men and women needs to be more widely manifested in the life of the Church.

Though they agree on this need, the churches draw different conclusions as to the admission of women to the ordained ministry. An increasing number of churches have decided that there is no biblical or theological reason against ordaining women, and many of them have subsequently proceeded to do so. Yet many churches hold that the tradition of the Church in this regard must not be changed.

© World Council of Churches, 1982.

From: Lambeth Palace London SE1 7JU
6th August 1988

The Transfiguration of Our Lord

To: His Holiness Pope John Paul II

Your Holiness,
At the close of the twelfth Lambeth Conference of the Bishops of the Anglican Communion, I write to you to thank you for the presence of the Catholic Observers, for your personal letter assuring the Conference of your prayers, and to inform you directly of the results of our deliberations.

One of the happy features of our Conference has been the presence of Observers and Speakers from many churches. Among the speakers it was a particular pleasure to welcome Father Pierre Duprey, Secretary of the Vatican Secretariat for Promoting Christian Unity, who delivered an important response to my own opening address. Father Duprey carried your letter to the Conference and I read it to the plenary assembly of

Bishops. The tactful courtesy in the manner of your reference to the known obstacle of the ordination of women was deeply appreciated.

Although the ordination of women to the priesthood and episcopate has been in the forefront of our deliberations, the principal issue before the Conference has actually been the underlying question of authority, the developing tradition of the Church, and ecclesiology. I spoke at some length to the Conference of this, including the structures required for unity: the episcopate, conciliarity and primacy. I spoke specifically of the primacy you demonstrated in Assisi in 1986 in convoking the Day of Prayer for Peace. Of your office as Bishop of Rome I asked:

"could not all Christians come to reconsider the kind of primacy exercised within the Early Church, a 'presiding in love' for the sake of the unity of the Churches"?

But the ecumenical pilgrimage has not yet reached this stage. In the meantime urgent questions have to be faced, new problems addressed and the mission of the Church exercised even in our separation. Thus in a number of Provinces of the Anglican Communion the question of the ordination of women to the priesthood, and now episcopate, arises. The Lambeth Conference has no juridical authority over the Anglican Communion. Nor do I. All the Provinces have the canonical authority to implement the mission of the Church as they deem right in their own culture. So the matter of the ordination of women, especially to the episcopate, has been deeply divisive.

Nevertheless, the overall ethos of the Lambeth Conference has been one of unity and communion despite deeply held differences. It is probable that some provinces, especially in North America, may shortly elect and consecrate a woman bishop. The Lambeth Conference resolved to respect this decision even if not all other bishops and provinces can yet recognize such a woman bishop. There will be the pain of some impairment of communion. Difficult as this is, it is, in the judgement of this Conference, a more acceptable solution than a schism within the Anglican Communion. We are now urgently to examine the relations between Provinces which differ in practice on this matter. We recognize the ecumenical implications of this debate but know that the Catholic Church would also see a split in the Anglican Communion as a grave ecumenical obstacle.

I acknowledge that there is need for much more study of the question of women's ordination. I also feel that this study should be conducted on an ecumenical basis. I was glad that this view was re-echoed in the response made to my opening address by Metropolitan John of Pergamos who is Co-Chairman of the Anglican/Orthodox dialogue and, of course, a member of the Catholic/Orthodox International Commission. He called for an exhaustive theological debate on this matter and said:

"It seems to me that we have not even begun to treat the issue of the ordination of women as a theological problem at an ecumenical level."

It is my prayer that such ecumenical debate, involving all Christians, may be taken up and carried out in an atmosphere of trust and mutual respect.

The Conference went on to consider the responses of 23 autonomous Provinces to the Final Report of the Anglican/Roman Catholic International Commission. One of the most important tasks of the Conference was to pronounce the consensus of the Anglican Communion on the Agreed Statements of the dialogue established by our predecessors in 1966. The Bishops, by a very large majority, recognized the ARCIC Agreed Statements on the eucharist and the ordained ministry as "consonant in substance with the faith of Anglicans".

On authority the Agreed Statements were welcomed as "a firm basis" for the future dialogue. The complete text of these very positive Resolutions is in the hands of the Catholic Observers. They represent a very strong affirmation by the Anglican Communion about the results of our dialogue.

While the Bishops of the Anglican Communion realize that there will be no easy solution to the difficult question of the ordination of women, I see this strong affirmation of the work of ARCIC-I as a significant Anglican step towards "the mutual recognition of the ministries of our two Communions" of which we spoke in Canterbury together in May 1982.

In spite of obstacles the Bishops of the Anglican Communion are determined to continue to seek the unity Our Lord wills and to pursue the quest for the full visible unity to which our two Communions are committed.

May God bestow upon us this gift and the grace to receive it.

Your Holiness' Brother in Christ,

Robert Cantuar

To The Most Reverend Robert Runcie
Archbishop of Canterbury

From the Vatican, 8th December 1988

I acknowledge with gratitude the letter which you sent to me at the close of the twelfth Lambeth Conference last August. Your thoughtfulness in informing me about the proceedings of the Conference is much appreciated. I see in this gracious gesture a further indication of the trust that exists between us and of the strong bond of communion by which we are already united.

In responding to your communication, I would first of all acknowledge the signs of openness to fuller communion with the Catholic Church which were evident at several points in the Conference, not least in your opening address and in the resolutions on the Final Report of ARCIC-1. At the same time, I must express my concern in respect of those developments at Lambeth which seem to have placed new obstacles in the way of reconciliation between Catholics and Anglicans. The Lambeth Conference's treatment of the question of women's ordination has created a new and perplexing situation for the members of the Second Anglican/Roman Catholic International Commission to whom, in 1982, we gave the mandate of studying "all that hinders the mutual recognition of the ministries of our Communions". The ordination of women to the priesthood in some provinces of the Anglican Communion, together with the recognition of the right of individual provinces to proceed with the ordination of women to the episcopacy, appears to preempt this study and effectively block the path to the mutual recognition of ministries.

The Catholic Church, like the Orthodox Church and the Ancient Oriental Churches, is firmly opposed to this development, viewing it as a break with Tradition of a kind we have no competence to authorize. It would seem that the discussion of women's ordination in the Anglican Communion has not taken sufficiently into account the ecumenical and ecclesiological dimensions of the question. Since the Anglican Communion is in dialogue with the Catholic Church–as it is with the Orthodox Church and the Ancient Oriental Churches–it is urgent that this aspect be given much greater attention in order to prevent a serious erosion of the degree of communion between us.

I am aware that no final decision on the controversial question of women's ordination has been taken as far as the Church of England is concerned. I likewise understand the delicate nature of your own position, given the autonomy of each of the provinces that make up the Anglican Communion, as well as your anxiety over a possible split within that Communion. Since, however, as Archbishop of Canterbury you also represent the Anglican Communion in its relations with the Catholic Church, a highly problematic situation could certainly arise for those provinces opposed to women's ordination if there were women priests in the Church of England. In addressing Your Grace so directly on this matter, I would stress that my motivation is simply to serve the quest for unity to which our predecessors Pope Paul VI and Archbishop Michael Ramsey committed themselves in 1966; a commitment which you and I renewed during my visit to Canterbury in 1982.

Assuring you of my prayers as we persevere in the search for that unity willed by the Lord for all his disciples, I renew my warm fraternal greetings in our Saviour Jesus Christ, the Eternal High Priest.

Joannes Paulus PPII

Apostolic Letter

Mulieris Dignitatem 1988

VII THE CHURCH-THE BRIDE OF CHRIST

The "great mystery"

23. Of fundamental importance here are the words of the Letter to the Ephesians: "Husbands, love your wives, as Christ loved the Church and gave himself up for her, that he might sanctify her, having cleansed her by the washing of water with the word, that he might present the Church to himself in splendour, without spot or wrinkle or any such thing, that she might be holy and without blemish. Even so husbands should love their wives as their own bodies. He who loves his wife loves himself. For no man ever hates his own flesh, but nourishes and cherishes it, as Christ does the Church, because we are members of his body. 'For this reason a man shall leave his father and mother and be joined to his wife, and the two shall become one flesh'. *This mystery is a profound one*, and I am saying that *it refers to Christ and the Church*" (5:25.32).

In this Letter the author expresses the truth about the Church as the bride of Christ, and also indicates how this truth *is rooted in the biblical reality of the creation of the human being as male and female*. Created in the image and likeness of God as a "unity of the two", both have been called to a spousal love. Following the description of creation in the Book of Genesis (2:18-25), one can also say that this fundamental call appears in the creation of woman, and is inscribed by the Creator in the institu-

tion of marriage, which, according to Genesis 2:24, has
the character of a union of persons (*"communio personar-
um"*) from the very beginning. Although not directly,
the very description of the "beginning" (cf. *Gen*
1:27;2:24) shows that the whole "ethos" of mutual
relations between men and women has to correspond to
the personal truth of their being.

All this has already been considered. The Letter to the
Ephesians once again confirms this truth, while at the
same time comparing the spousal character of the love
between man and woman to the mystery of Christ and
of the Church. *Christ is the Bridegroom of the Church-the
Church is the Bride of Christ.* This analogy is not without
precedent; it transfers to the New Testament what was
already contained *in the Old Testament*, especially in the
prophets Hosea, Jeremiah, Ezekiel and Isaiah.[1] The
respective passages deserve a separate analysis. Here we
will cite only one text. This is how God speaks to his
Chosen People through the Prophet: "Fear not, for you
will not be ashamed; be not confounded, for you will
not be put to shame; for you will forget the shame of
your youth, and the reproach of your widowhood you
will remember no more. *For your Maker is your husband*,
the Lord of hosts is his name; and the Holy One of Israel
is *your Redeemer*, the God of the whole earth he is called.
For the Lord has called you like a wife forsaken and
grieved in spirit, like a wife of youth when she is cast
off, says your God. For a brief moment I forsook you,
but with great compassion I will gather you. In
overflowing wrath for a moment I hid my face from
you, but with everlasting love I will have compassion
on you, says the Lord, your Redeemer. ...For the
mountains may depart and the hills be removed, *but my
steadfast love shall not depart from you*, and my covenant of
peace shall not be removed, says the Lord, who has
compassion on you" (Is 54:4-8, 10).

Since the human being-man and woman-has been

created in God's image and likeness, God can speak
about himself through the lips of the Prophet using
language which is essentially human. In the text of
Isaiah quoted above, the expression of God's love is
"human", but the *love* itself *is divine*. Since it is God's
love, its spousal character is properly divine, even
though it is expressed by the analogy of a man's love for
a woman. The woman-bride is Israel, God's Chosen
People, and this choice originates exclusively in God's
gratuitous love. It is precisely this love which explains
the Covenant, a Covenant often presented as a marriage
covenant which God always renews with his Chosen
People. On the part of God the Covenant is a lasting
"commitment"; he remains faithful to his spousal love
even if the bride often shows herself to be unfaithful.

This *image of spousal love*, together with the figure of
the divine Bridegroom-a very clear image in the texts of
the Prophets-finds crowning confirmation in the Letter
to the Ephesians (5:23-32). *Christ* is greeted as the
bridegroom by John the Baptist (cf. *Jn* 3:27-29). Indeed
Christ applies to himself this comparison drawn from
the Prophets (cf. *Mk* 2:19-20). The Apostle Paul, who is
a bearer of the Old Testament heritage, writes to the
Corinthians: "I feel a divine jealousy for you, for I
betrothed you to Christ to present you as a pure bride to
her one husband" (2 *Cor* 11:2). But the fullest expression of the truth about Christ the Redeemer's love,
according to the analogy of spousal love in marriage, is
found in the Letter to the Ephesians: *"Christ loved the
Church and gave himself up for her"* (5:25), thereby fully
confirming the fact that the Church is the bride of
Christ: "The Holy One of Israel is your Redeemer" (*Is*
54:5). In Saint Paul's text the analogy of the spousal
relationship moves simultaneously in two directions
which make up the whole of the "great mystery"
(*"sacramentum magnum"*). The covenant proper to
spouses "explains" the spousal character of the union of

Christ with the Church, and in its turn this union, as a "great sacrament", determines the sacramentality of marriage as a holy covenant between the two spouses, man and woman. Reading this rich and complex passage, which *taken as a whole is a great analogy*, we must *distinguish* that element which expresses the human reality of interpersonal relations from that which expresses in symbolic language the "great mystery" which is divine.

The Gospel "innovation"

24. The text is addressed to the spouses as real women and men. It reminds them of the "ethos" of spousal love which goes back to the divine institution of marriage from the "beginning". Corresponding to the truth of this institution is the exhortation: "*Husbands, love your wives*", love them because of that special and unique bond whereby in marriage a man and a woman become "one flesh" (*Gen* 2:24; *Eph* 5:31). In this love there is a fundamental *affirmation of the woman* as a person. This affirmation makes it possible for the female personality to develop fully and be enriched. This is precisely the way Christ acts as the bridegroom of the Church: he desires that she be "in splendour, without spot or wrinkle" (*Eph* 5:27). One can say that this fully captures the whole "style" of Christ in dealing with women. Husbands should make their own the elements of this style in regard to their wives, analogously, all men should do the same in regard to women in every situation. In this way both men and women bring about "the sincere gift of self".

The author of the Letter to the Ephesians sees no contradiction between an exhortation formulated in this way and the words: "Wives, be subject to your husbands, as to the Lord. For the husband is the head of the wife" (5:22-23). The author knows that this way of speaking, so profoundly rooted in the customs and religious tradition of the time, is to be understood and carried out in a new way: as a *"mutual subjection out of reverence for Christ" (cf. Eph* 5:21). This is especially true because the husband is called the "head" of the wife *as* Christ is the head of the Church; he is so in order to give "himself up for her" (*Eph* 5:25), and giving himself up for her means giving up even his own life. However, whereas in the relationship between Christ and the Church the subjection is only on the part of the Church, in the relationship between husband and wife the "subjection" is not one-sided but mutual.

In relation to the "old" this is evidently something "new": it is an innovation of the Gospel. We find various passages in which the apostolic writings express this innovation, even though they also communicate what is "old": what is rooted in the religious tradition of Israel, in its way of understanding and explaining the sacred texts, as for example the second chapter of the Book of Genesis.[2]

The apostolic letters are addressed to people living in an environment marked by the same traditional way of thinking and acting. The "innovation" of Christ is a fact: it constitutes the unambiguous content of the evangelical message and is the result of the Redemption. However, the awareness that in marriage there is mutual "subjection of the spouses out of reverence for Christ", and not just that of the wife to the husband, must gradually establish itself in hearts, consciences, behaviour and customs. This is a call which from that time onwards, does not cease to challenge succeeding generations; it is a call which people have to accept ever anew. Saint Paul not only wrote: "In Christ Jesus- ...there is no more man or woman", but also wrote: "There is no more slave or freeman". Yet how many generations were needed for such a principle to be realized in the history of humanity through the abolition of slavery! And what is one to say of the many forms of slavery to which individuals and peoples are subjected, which have not yet disappeared from history?

But *the challenge presented by the "ethos" of the Redemption* is clear and definitive. All the reasons in favour of the "subjection" of woman to man in marriage must be understood in the sense of a "mutual subjection" of both "out of reverence for Christ". The measure of true spousal love finds its deepest source in Christ, who is the Bridegroom of the Church, his Bride.

The symbolic dimension of the "great mystery"
25.In the Letter to the Ephesians we encounter *a second dimension* of the analogy which, taken as a whole, serves to reveal the "great mystery". This is *a symbolic dimension*. If God's love for the human person, for the Chosen People of Israel, is presented by the Prophets as the love of the bridegroom for the bride, such an analogy expresses the "spousal" quality and the divine and non-human character of God's love: "For your Maker is your husband...the God of the whole earth he is called" (*Is* 54:5). The same can also be said of the spousal love of Christ the Redeemer: "For God so loved the world that he gave his only Son" (*Jn* 3:16). It is a matter, therefore, of God's love expressed by means of the Redemption accomplished by Christ. According to Saint Paul's Letter, this love is "like" the spousal love of human spouses, but naturally it is not "the same". For the analogy implies a likeness, while at the same time leaving ample room for non-likeness.

This is easily seen in regard to the person of the "bride". According to the Letter of the Ephesians, the bride *is the Church*, just as for the Prophets the bride was Israel. She is therefore *a collective subject* and not *an individual person*. This collective subject is the People of God, a community made up of many persons, both women and men. "Christ has loved the Church" precisely as a community, as the People of God. At the same time, in this Church, which in the same passage is also called his "body" (cf. *Eph* 5:23), he has loved every individual person. For Christ has redeemed all without exception, every man and woman. It is precisely this love of God which is expressed in the Redemption; the spousal character of this love reaches completion in the history of humanity and of the world.

Christ has entered this history and remains in it as the Bridegroom who "has given himself". "To give" means "to become a sincere gift" in the most complete and radical way: "Greater love has no man than this" (*Jn* 15:13). According to this conception, *all human beings- both women and men-are called* through the Church, *to be the "Bride" of Christ, the Redeemer of the world*. In this way "being the bride", and thus the "feminine" element, becomes a symbol of all that is "human", according to the words of Paul: "There is neither male nor female: for you are all, *one* in Christ Jesus" (*Gal* 3:28).

From a linguistic viewpoint we can say that the analogy of spousal love found in the Letter to the Ephesians links what is "masculine" to what is "feminine", since, as members of the Church, men too are included in the concept of "Bride". This should not surprise us, for Saint Paul, in order to express his mission in Christ and in the Church, speaks of the "little children with whom he is again in travail" (cf. *Gal* 4:19). In the sphere of what is "human"-of what is humanly personal- *"masculinity" and "femininity" are distinct*, yet at the same time they *complete and explain each other*. This is also present in the great analogy of the "Bride" in the Letter to the Ephesians. In the Church every human being-male and female- is the "Bride", in that he or she accepts the gift of the love of Christ the Redeemer, and seeks to respond to it with the gift of his or her own person.

Christ is the Bridegroom. This expresses the truth about the love of God who "first loved us" (cf. 1 *Jn* 4:19) and who, with the gift generated by this spousal love for man, has exceeded all human expectations: "He loved them to the end" (*Jn* 13:1). The Bridegroom-the Son consubstantial with the Father as God-became the son of Mary; he became the "son of man", true man, a male. *The symbol of the Bridegroom is masculine*. This masculine symbol represents the human aspect of the divine love which God has for Israel, for the Church, and for all people. Meditating on what the Gospels say about Christ's attitude towards women, we can conclude that *as a man*, a son of Israel, he *revealed* the dignity of the "daughters of Abraham" (cf. *Lk* 13:16), *the dignity belonging to women* from the very "beginning" on an equal footing with men. At the same time Christ emphasized the originality which distinguishes women from men, all the richness lavished upon women in the mystery of creation. Christ's attitude towards women serves as a model of what the Letter to the Ephesians expresses with the concept of "bridegroom". Precisely because Christ's divine love is the love of a Bridegroom, it is the model and pattern of all human love, men's love in particular.

The Eucharist

26. Against the broad background of the "great mystery" expressed in the spousal relationship between Christ and the Church, it is possible to understand adequately the calling of the "Twelve". *In calling only men as his Apostles*, Christ acted *in a completely free and sovereign manner*. In doing so, he exercised the same freedom with which, in all his behaviour, he emphasized the dignity and the vocation of women, without conforming to the prevailing customs and to the traditions sanctioned by the legislation of the time. Consequently, the assumption that he called men to be

apostles in order to conform with the widespread mentality of his times, does not at all correspond to Christ's way of acting. "Teacher, we know that you are true, and teach the way of God truthfully, and care for no man; for *you do not regard the position of men*" (Mt 22:16). These words fully characterize *Jesus of Nazareth's behaviour*. Here one also finds an explanation for the calling of the "Twelve". They are with Christ at the Last Supper. They alone receive the sacramental charge. "Do this in remembrance of me" (*Lk* 22:19; 1 *Cor* 11:24), which is joined to the institution of the Eucharist. On Easter Sunday night they receive the Holy Spirit for the forgiveness of sins: "Whose sins you forgive are forgiven them, and whose sins you retain are retained" (*Jn* 20:23).

We find ourselves at the very heart of the Paschal Mystery, which completely reveals the spousal love of God. Christ is the Bridegroom because "he has given himself": his body has been "given", his blood has been "poured out" (cf. *Lk* 22:19-20). In this way "he loved them to the end" (*Jn* 13:1). The "sincere gift" contained in the Sacrifice of the Cross gives definitive prominence to the spousal meaning of God's love. As the Redeemer of the world, Christ is the Bridegroom of the Church. *The Eucharist* is *the Sacrament of our Redemption*. It is *the Sacrament of the Bridegroom and of the Bride*. The Eucharist makes present and realizes anew in a sacramental manner the redemptive act of Christ, who "creates", the Church, his body. Christ is united with this "body" as the bridegroom with the bride. All this is contained in the Letter to the Ephesians. The perennial "unity of the two" that exists between man and woman from the very "beginning" is introduced into this "great mystery" of Christ and of the Church.

Since Christ, in instituting the Eucharist, linked it in such an explicit way to the priestly service of the Apostles, it is legitimate to conclude that he thereby wished to express the relationship between man and woman, between what is "feminine" and what is "masculine". It is a relationship willed by God both in the mystery of creation and in the mystery of Redemption. It is *the Eucharist* above all that expresses *the redemptive act of Christ the Bridegroom towards the Church the Bride*. This is clear and unambiguous when the sacramental ministry of the Eucharist, in which the priest acts *"in persona Christi"*, is performed by a man. This explanation confirms the teaching of the Declaration *Inter Insigniores*, published at the behest of Paul VI in response to the question concerning the admission of women to the ministerial priesthood.[3]

The Gift of the Bride
27. The Second Vatican Council renewed the Church's awareness of the universality of the priesthood. In the New Covenant there is only one sacrifice and only one priest: Christ. *All the baptized share in the one priesthood of Christ*, both men and women, inasmuch as they must "present their bodies as a living sacrifice, holy and acceptable to God (cf. *Rom* 12:1), give witness to Christ in every place, and give an explanation to anyone who asks the reason for the hope in eternal life that is in them (cf. 1 *Pt* 3:15)".[4] Universal participation in Christ's sacrifice, in which the Redeemer has offered to the Father the whole world and humanity in particular, brings it about that all in the Church are "a kingdom of priests" (*Rev* 5:10; cf. 1 *Pt* 2:9), who not only share in the priestly mission but also in the prophetic and kingly mission of Christ the Messiah. Furthermore, this participation determines the organic unity of the Church, the People of God, with Christ. It expresses at the same time the "great mystery" described in the Letter to the Ephesians: *the bride united to her Bridegroom*; united, because she lives his life; united, because she shares in his threefold mission (*tria munera Christi*);

united *in such a manner as to respond* with a "sincere gift" of self *to the inexpressible gift of the love of the Bridegroom*, the Redeemer of the world. This concerns everyone in the Church, women as well as men. It obviously concerns those who share in the "ministerial priesthood",[5] which is characterized by service. In the context of the "great mystery" of Christ and of the Church, all are called to respond-as a bride-with the gift of their lives to the inexpressible gift of the love of Christ, who alone, as the Redeemer of the world, is the Church's Bridegroom. The "royal priesthood", which is universal, at the same time expresses the gift of the Bride.

This is of *fundamental importance for understanding the Church in her own essence*, so as to avoid applying to the Church-even in her dimension as an "institution" made up of human beings and forming part of history-criteria of understanding and judgement which do not pertain to her nature. Although the Church possesses a "hierarchical" structure,[6] nevertheless this structure is totally ordered to the holiness of Christ's members. And holiness is measured according to the "great mystery" in which the Bride responds with the gift of love to the gift of the Bridegroom. She does this "in the Holy Spirit", since "God's love has been poured into our hearts through the Holy Spirit who has been given to us" (*Rom* 5:5). The Second Vatican Council, confirming the teaching of the whole of tradition, recalled that in the hierarchy of holiness it is *precisely the "woman"*, Mary of Nazareth, who is the "figure" of the Church. She "precedes" everyone on the path to holiness; in her person "the Church has already reached that perfection whereby she exists without spot or wrinkle (cf. *Eph* 5:27)".[7]. In this sense, one can say that the Church is *both* "Marian" and "Apostolic-Petrine".[8]

In the history of the Church, even from earliest times, there were side-by-side with men *a number of women*, for whom the response of the Bride to the Bridegroom's redemptive love acquired full expressive force. First we see those women who had personally encountered Christ and followed him. After his departure, together with the Apostles, they "devoted themselves to prayer" in the Upper Room in Jerusalem until the day of Pentecost. On that day the Holy Spirit spoke through "the sons and daughters" of the People of God, thus fulfilling the words of the prophet Joel (cf. *Acts* 2:17). These women, and others afterwards, played *an active and important role in the life of the early Church*, in building up from its foundations the first Christian community-and subsequent communities-*through their own charisms and their varied service*. The apostolic writings note their names, such as Phoebe, "a deaconess of the Church at Cenchreae" (cf. *Rom* 16:1), Prisca with her husband Aquila (cf. 2 *Tim* 4:19), Euodia and Syntyche (cf. *Phil* 4:2), Mary, Tryphaena, Persis, and Tryphosa (cf. *Rom* 16:6, 12). Saint Paul speaks of their "hard work" for Christ, and this hard work indicates the various fields of the Church's apostolic service, beginning with the "domestic Church". For in the latter, "sincere faith" passes from the mother to her children and grandchildren, as was the case in the house of Timothy (cf. 2 *Tim* 1:5).

The same thing is repeated down the centuries, from one generation to the next, as *the history of the Church* demonstrates. By defending the dignity of women and their vocation, the Church has shown honour and gratitude for those women who-faithful to the Gospel-have shared in every age in the apostolic mission of the whole People of God. They are the holy martyrs, virgins, and mothers of families, who bravely bore witness to their faith and passed on the Church's faith and tradition by bringing up their children in the spirit of the Gospel.

In every age and in every country we find many

"perfect" women (cf. *Prov*. 31:10) who, despite persecution, difficulties and discrimination have shared in the Church's mission. It suffices to mention: Monica, the mother of Augustine, Macrina, Olga of Kiev, Matilda of Tuscany, Hedwig of Silesia, Jadwiga of Cracow, Elizabeth of Thuringia, Birgitta of Sweden, Joan of Arc, Rose of Lima, Elizabeth Ann Seton and Mary Ward.

The witness and the achievements of Christian women have had a significant impact on the life of the Church as well as of society. Even in the face of serious social discriminatiion, holy women have acted "freely", strengthened by their union with Christ. Such union and freedom rooted in God explain, for example, the great work of Saint Catherine of Siena in the life of the Church, and the work of Saint Teresa of Jesus in the monastic life.

In our own days too the Church is constantly enriched by the witness of the many women who fulfil their vocation to holiness. Holy women are an incarnation of the feminine ideal; they are also a model for all Christians, a model of the *"sequela Christi"*, an example of how the Bride must respond with love to the love of the Bridegroom.

Notes.

1. Cf. for example, *Hos* 1:2; 2:16–18; *Jer* 2:2; *Ezek* 16:8; *Is* 50:1; 54:5–8.
2. Cf. *Col* 3:18; 1 *Pt* 3:1–6; *Tit* 2:4–5; *Eph* 5:22–24; 1 *Cor* 11:3–16; 14:33–35; 1 *Tim* 2:11–15
3. Cf. Congregation for the Doctrine of the Faith. Declaration Concerning the Question of the Admission of Women to the Ministerial Priesthood *Inter Insigniores* (15 October 1976): *AAS* 69 (1977), 98–116.
4. Cf. Second Vatican Ecumenical Council. Dogmatic Constitution on the Church *Lumen Gentium*, 10.
5. Cf. *ibid.*, 10.
6. Cf. *ibid.*, 18–29.
7. *Ibid.*, 65; cf. also 63; cf. Encyclical Letter *Redemptoris Mater*, 2–6: *loc. cit.*, 362–367.
8. "This *Marian* profile is also–even perhaps more so–fundamental and characteristic for the Church as is the *apostolic* and *Petrine* profile to which it is profoundly united. … The Marian dimension of the Church

is antecedent to that of the Petrine, without being in any way divided from it or being less complementary. Mary Immaculate precedes all others, including obviously Peter himself and the Apostles. This is so, not only because Peter and the Apostles, being born of the human race under the burden of sin, form part of the Church which is 'holy from out of sinners', but also because their triple *function* has no other purpose except to form the Church in line with the ideal of sanctity already programmed and prefigured in Mary. A contemporary theologian has rightly stated that Mary is 'Queen of the Apostles without any pretensions to apostolic powers: she has other and greater powers' (H.U. von Balthasar, *Neue Klarstellungen)"*. *Address* to the Cardinals and Prelates of the Roman Curia (22 December 1987): *L'Osservatore Romano*, 23 December 1987.

The Place of the Woman in the Orthodox Church and the Question of the Ordination of Women

I THEOLOGICAL APPROACHES

2. *The priesthood of Christ*

As the head of the Church, Christ is forever the only Mediator and great High Priest. For the means of His whole work of salvation and His sacrifice, He reconciled humanity to God (2 Cor 5:18-20). Through the grace of the Sacraments in the Church, the Holy Spirit testifies to the continuity of the presence and mediation of Christ, through which the faithful are constituted "children of God", "heirs of God and co-heirs with Christ". "All have received the Spirit of adoption" (Romans 8:15-17) and all have been made members of the body of Christ (1 Corinthians 12:17, Ephesians 4:25, 5:30), "conformed to the likeness of the Son" (Romans 8:29) and have become the "people of God" (1 Peter 2:10). All the faithful then, are able to participate "in accordance to the measure of the faith" which they have (Romans 12:3-8) in the gifts (charismata) of the Holy Spirit and in the varied ministries (diakoniai) in the body of the Church (Acts 1:17 and 24, Romans 12:2, 1 Corinthians 12:5, 2 Corinthians 4:1, Ephesians 4:12, Colossians 4:17, 1 Timothy 1:12, 2 Timothy 4:5). The sacramental Priesthood is a distinctive charisma of the Holy Spirit. It unifies all of the gifts (charismata) and all of the ministries (diakoniai) in the Church. The Lord remains forever the great High Priest and the sole celebrant of the Sacraments.

Among the many gifts of the Spirit in the life of the Church is the "sacerdotal" or "special" Priesthood. Granted by the Lord Himself, the sacramental Priesthood leads, nurtures and builds up the body of believers. It was given by the Lord to the Apostles and to their successors in the apostolic ministry of *episkope* for the people of God. This sacramental Priesthood, iconically presenting Christ, as the head of the body, is granted to the Church through the grace of the Holy Spirit at the sacrament of ordination (Cheirotonia) by which those being ordained are made "servants of Christ and stewards of the mysteries of God" (1 Cor 4:1).

Jesus Christ gives this special Priesthood to the Apostles and to their successors. The consciousness of the Church from the very beginning excluded women from participation in this special priesthood, on the basis of the example of the Lord and the Apostolic tradition and practice, in the light of the Pauline teaching concerning the relationship of the male and female in the new reality in Christ (1 Cor 11:3).

3. The Typology of "Adam-Christ" and "Eve-Mary"

This distinction in the relationship of man and woman in regard to the sacramental Priesthood according to the "order of nature", flows from the deeper understanding of the relation of men and women in the plan of salvation in Christ, yet it was never, in any case, understood in the Orthodox tradition as a diminution of the role of women in the Church. In the mystery of the whole divine Economy of salvation, women are understood as equally sharing with men in the *image of God*, and as being of equal honour with men. As such, women in the Church assume their own roles for the restoration of the distorted image of God, which are a consequence of sin.

The distinct role of women is expressed by means of

the typological analogy "Eve-Mary" and by means of the special relationship of women to the distinct work of the Holy Spirit in the whole plan of salvation in Christ. The typological relationship "Adam-Christ", by means of which Adam is the prefiguration of Christ on the one hand, while Christ - being the New Adam - is the model of the old Adam who recapitulates the human race, is foundational to the whole Patristic theology and life of the Church. Consistent with this, the typology determines the special content of the ministry of women in the work of the realization of the recapitulation of the New Adam and the salvation of the whole human race.

The central person in the special ministry of women in the divine plan of salvation is the Theotokos, the Mother of God. In her is fulfilled the special work of the Holy Spirit for the Incarnation of the Son and Word of God. The typological relationship moving from Mary to Eve was necessary for the release of the bonds of Eve and the Incarnation of the Son and Word of God, through the Holy Spirit and Mary. Thus, while on the one hand Eve "being disobedient, became the cause of death, for herself and all of humanity", on the other hand, the Virgin Mary, "being obedient, became the cause of salvation for herself and for all of humanity" (Irenaeus *Adv. Haer.* III, 24; 3, 4). So in this manner, Eve represents fallen ancient humanity, while the Theotokos represents the transfiguration of that ancient fallen humanity, through the birth in Christ of the new humanity.

This ministry of woman was fulfilled through the creative descent upon the Virgin Mary of the Holy Spirit, which became a new locus (topos) "for the power of the Most High which descended upon her." The Spirit cleansed her and granted to her the necessary "creative ability" (gennetiken dynamin) through the wondrous incarnation of the Son and Word of God which took place through her. Thus, the Virgin Mary, at the Annunciation, became the receptor of the epiphany of the Holy Spirit for the fulfilment of the typological reclamation by Mary of Eve (tes apo tes Marias eis ten Evan ankykleseos), and through the incarnation of the New Adam who recapitulates in Himself all things. This relationship between the special work of the Holy Spirit and the Virgin Mary, and the typological relationship of the Old and New Adam in history thus provides us with important insights into the Church's approach to the issue of man and women in regard to ordination to the sacramental Priesthood.

4. The Male Character of the "Sacramental" Priesthood

The Theotokos has been presented to us as the type of the Church. The Church, like the Theotokos receives the Holy Spirit, through whose energy both Christ is born and, also, the children of the new humanity in Christ are brought into the world. Thus, in the patristic tradition, there is presented the typological relationship of the motherhood of the Theotokos and the motherhood of the Church. The special functional relationship of the role of the Theotokos with the work of the Holy Spirit in the incarnation is extended to and lived in the age of the Church.

This typological relationship provides the foundation – through the example of the Theotokos – of the general content of the consciousness of the Church concerning the impossibility of ordaining women to the Christocentric sacramental Priesthood. (Apostolic Constitutions III, 6,1-2, 9,1-4. Tertullian, De Virginibus Vel., 9,1. Epiphanios, Against Heresies, 59, 2-3. PG 42, 741-744). Whenever this ecclesiological consciousness is changed, it creates serious ecclesiological problems. These have appeared in the past, and today they are clear in the ecclesiology of those who support the ordination of women to the special priesthood. This is so precisely because this change in ecclesiology weakens the patristic teaching regarding the balance in the Church of Christology in relation to Pneumatology.

Thus, the impossibility of the ordination of women to the special priesthood as founded in the tradition of the Church has been expressed in these ecclesiastically rooted positions:

(a) on the example of our Lord Jesus Christ, who did not select any woman as one of His Apostles;
(b) on the example of the Theotokos, who did not exercise the sacramental priestly function in the Church, even though she was made worthy to become the mother of the Incarnate Son and Word of God;
(c) on the Apostolic Tradition, according to which the Apostles, following the example of the Lord, never ordained any women to this special Priesthood of episcope in the Church;
(d) on some Pauline teachings concerning the position of women in the Church;
(e) on the criterion of analogy, according to which, if the exercise of episcope by women were permitted, then it should have been exercised by the Theotokos.

5. Christ and the Theotokos in the Recapitulation of Humanity

Jesus Christ is the saviour of all persons, both men and women. Yet, in the typological and iconic experience of worship and the pastoral life of the Church, Christ as the High Priest is presented to us appropriately and fittingly only by a male in the High Priestly image. Conversely, the Theotokos, the Mother of God, represents all of humanity, both female and male in the divine act of the incarnation, giving to the eternal Son of God his human nature. She is the Mother of us all, especially the members of the Body of the Church. As such, the Theotokos, in the typological and iconic experience of worship and the whole experience of the Christian life, presents us before the Lord's throne in a way which uniquely speaks for us as creatures of God.

All Christians, women and men, must come into personal communion with Christ, who shows no discrimination toward us, for He is the Saviour of each and all in total disregard of any humanly based discriminations. Just as Orthodox Christians, men and women, find in the first of all Saints, the Theotokos, the person who gave the flesh and soul of humanity to the Son and Word of God for His incarnation, A "ready help", and "intercessor" and a "true mother of all Christians".

However, in the typology of worship the unbroken tradition of the Church, with no exception at all, has called upon only certain men to serve at the Altar as Priests who iconically present to the Body of Christ her head and Lord, the High Priest Jesus Christ. In like fashion, the female figure of the Theotokos is the typological representation of all the People of God. The representative and intercessory place of the Theotokos is made manifest in the iconographic cycle in Orthodox architecture, according to which the icon of the Theotokos holding the Christ in her lap (Platytera), dominates the liturgical space over the Altar Table. Thus, in the iconic and typological framework of worship, the male figure is appropriate to the High Priestly role, and the female figure of the Virgin appropriately models the Church for all of the members of the Body.

We are here not simply dealing with theological concepts and ideas. We are in a sphere of profound, almost indescribable experience of the inner ethos of the world-saving and cosmic dimensions of Christian truth. The iconic and typological mode of dealing with the issue tells us that rational constructs will not be adequate alone to describe and express it fully. Like all of the mysteries of the Faith as lived in Orthodox, this one too, is articulated with the fear of God and with a sense of reverence. Yet, deep in the inner workings of the ethos and tradition of the Church, we sense that our words are words of truth and not mere apologetics, and that ignoring the reality of which they speak will not only deny the past reality of the Church, but will deprive all who do so of foundational and essential dimensions of the full Christian experience of life in Christ.

II SPECIAL CONCERNS

6. *The Equality of Women and Men and the Distinctiveness of Women and Men*

As was noted above, the Orthodox understanding both of God and the human person is rooted in the fact of divine revelation. The manner in which we approach God, and the way we understand women and men is not left solely to our limited reason, valuable that it is. Rather, God has acted to provide us with insight into who he is and to who we are (Ps 118:27).

Because of the divine revelation, which is centred upon the Incarnation of our Lord, the Orthodox would affirm the following features as central to our understanding of men and women. Firstly, God is the creator of both men and women. Each has his or her origin with God. This conviction is further strengthened by our acknowledgement that Christ has come to save men and women equally and to restore both men and women to fellowship with God (Col 1:20).

Of equal significance is the Orthodox conviction expressed throughout the Scriptures and Tradition of the Church that there is a distinction between the male and the female which is rooted in the very act of creation (Gen 1:27). This distinction does not imply any form of inferiority or superiority before God. On the contrary, it is a distinction established by God Himself as part of his divine plan. Salvation does not involve, therefore, the denial of our identity as women and men but rather its transfiguration.

Witnessing the tragic dehumanization which we often encounter in our society, the Orthodox are bound to affirm in the strongest possible way the dignity of the human person, both the female and the male. Any act which denies the dignity of the human person and any act which discriminates against women and men on the basis of gender is a sin. It is therefore the task of the Church to affirm before the world the dignity of the human person, created in the image and likeness of God (Gen 1:26).

7. *Fuller Participation of Women in the Life of the Church*

With spiritual discernment throughout the centuries, the Church has encouraged the Christian woman to practice, together with men and in accordance with her nature and her personal inclinations and vocations, a whole variety of ministries. These have been in the area of liturgical, pastoral, catechetical, didactic, missionary, and social work. Special attention should be paid to female Monasticism for the manner in which it has contributed to the advancement of the position of women in the Church in particularly difficult circumstances.

While recognizing these facts, which witness to the promotion through the Church of the equality of honour between men and women, it is necessary to confess in honesty and with humility:

that owing to human weakness and sinfulness, the Christian communities have not always and in all places been able to suppress effectively ideas, manners and customs, historical developments and social conditions which have resulted in practical discrimination against women. Human sinfulness has thus led to practices which do not reflect the true nature of the Church of Jesus Christ.

Therefore, it is necessary that the fullness of truth should be constantly preserved through intense and unceasing prayer, calling upon the Divine assistance for "discernment of spirits" (1 John 4:1) and interpreting the true meaning of "the signs of the times" (Mt 16:3). Only thus the Church will be able to re-order her ability to walk according to the will of God and to declare his Kingdom each particular time and in each particular place.

The Church should re-examine potential data, views and actions, which do not agree with her unshakable theological and ecclesiological principles, but have intruded from outside and, being in fact perpetuated, may be interpreted as demeaning towards women.

Moreover, the necessity for a specific delimitation of roles in the Church should be emphasized, especially in matters pertaining to ecclesiastical organisation. The Orthodox stress spiritual authority rather than temporal power. When we speak about authority in the Church, we are in no way advocating a sort of bureaucratic organizational clericalism but rather we are emphasizing a special charism in the Church.

It follows that when we speak of roles in the Church, we speak of special gifts of the Spirit to be received with gratitude rather than of what may be interpreted as administrative "ranks" to be enforced by a hierarchical structure. We would here note the importance of highlighting the pastoral dimension that is ours to address issues raised by Orthodox women. These fall within the therapeutic function of the community manifested in different tasks entrusted to its members.

We would also underline the importance of the actual work which women are undertaking at the parish level today, but often without sufficient support and encouragement from the leadership of the Church. Among such tasks we would note the following:

(a) Education and Christian nurture at all levels ranging from Church schools to higher theological education in seminaries.

(b) Pastoral counselling of married couples, families, preparation for marriage, preparation for baptism, and care of people in situations of distress.

(c) Church administration, the participation in decision-making bodies at the level of the parish, the diocese and the national church.

(d) Social service including working with the elderly, hospital work, working with the deprived and the neglected.

(e) Choir directors, readers, singers

(f) Iconography

(g) Youth work

(h) Representation in the various aspects of the ecumenical movement

(i) Publications/communications.

All these tasks are to be seen as supportive diaconia, a complementary pastoral dimension in harmony with the specific sacerdotal ministry of the clergy.

We would also make special reference to the fact that the increasing number of women who are graduates of theology and other fields of advanced study in certain Churches creates a new reality which the Church is called to consider constructively. The zeal, the faith and the dedication of many of these women could effectively contribute to the renewal of parish life and church life as a whole, especially if greater attention were paid to them and if the undertaking on their part of their charismatic and theological ability in their work of teaching in their ministry and pastoral care for the people were blessed through a special ecclesiastical act. The same applies to a greater degree for able and charismatic nuns, who, alongside the practice of asceticism in the monastery could be present in the parish and care for special needs of the Church militant. Similarly, the wife of the priest exercises a distinctive ministry. Special attention should be given to her vocation as it exists within contemporary society.

All the above, and all other related matters, connected with the place of the woman and more generally of the laity in the Church, regarding their active participation in the various church services and ministries, should become the object of further study by Theological Schools and specialized researchers. To this end would contribute positively the more regular convocation of theological meetings and consultations, such as the present one, and would promote our spiritual cooperation and participation in the trials and hope of the Church.

Archbishop of Canterbury's Commission Report 1989

III. *Koinonia and Women in the Episcopate*

35. The churches of the Anglican Communion live out their life of worship, witness and work in increasingly diverse circumstances. It is entirely natural that these varied contexts should affect the Church's perceptions of what is required to sustain and to extend the mission of the Church in each particular context and in the world as a whole. Bishops of African origin, meeting in Cambridge, England, just before the Lambeth Conference, 1988, declared that it was their hope that the bishops, gathered together at Lambeth, would focus their attention on issues such as poverty, famine, Third World debt, the abuse of human rights, refugees, the drug and arms trades, moral education in society, and inculturation. In addition, there was widespread concern about evangelization and this culminated in several resolutions of the conference urging the Anglican Communion to shift its emphasis from pastoral care to mission, including programmes of evangelization.

36. The preparatory material for the Lambeth Conference 1988, and the Conference itself, squarely placed the question of the ordination of women to the priesthood and episcopate in the context of the Church's mission. The Conference recognised that the desire to ordain women arises from a perception that the ordination of women is necessary for the credibility of the Church in a

particular context; in other words, that it is necessary for mission. Provinces which have ordained women have done so because they believe that the mission of the Church in their context demands such a course of action. At the same time, the report of the Conference recognizes that a decision not to ordain women may also be taken for reasons having to do with the mission of the Church in a particular context. There are, however, some who oppose the ordination of women not primarily for missionary reasons but because of their understanding of apostolic Tradition. Some of these may see that the ordination of women enhances the credibility of the Church in certain contexts but they do not feel free to endorse such a development in the Church's Tradition without the agreement of all the churches claiming to possess the historic ministry, or at least of the Anglican Communion as a whole.

37. In Provinces considering or presently ordaining women to the priesthood and episcopate there has been considerable debate as to the appropriate way of ensuring pastoral and sacramental care for dissenting minorities for whom this development is not only undesirable but also unacceptable. Discussion has focussed on the question of extra diocesan episcopal care for congregations unwilling to receive the pastoral care of a woman bishop or priest.

38. Some proposals amount to a separate and parallel episcopal jurisdiction within the same territory. We note that Provinces have been unenthusiastic about such radical suggestions. Indeed, successive Lambeth Conferences have set their face against parallel Anglican jurisdictions. Even where they exist-as in continental Europe-they have been consistently deplored (cf eg, Lambeth Conference, 1897, Res. 24; Lambeth Conference, 1968, Res. 63). Suspicion of parallel jurisdictions seems soundly based in an ecclesiology of 'communion' which sees the bishop as the sacramental representative

of the whole local ecclesial community, and that community itself as truly grounded in its social context and culture. The classical definition of schism was indeed the setting up of rival episcopal thrones in the same local community.

39. Against this it must be noted that the Anglican Communion has more recently accepted the practice of parallel 'cultural' jurisdictions; as, for example, in the diocese of Aotearoa in New Zealand, the Order of Ethiopia in Southern Africa, and the Navajoland Area Mission in the USA. In Europe the two Iberian Churches are extra provincial to Canterbury, while the diocese in Europe is organized quite separately as a diocese 'within' the Province of Canterbury.

40. Yet these hardly offer possible models because such parallel jurisdictions remain in communion with each other and there is no theoretical problem about the interchangeability of ministries. They have usually been described as being in 'full communion'. While the Polish National Catholic Church in the U.S.A. has declared itself to be no longer in 'full communion' with the Episcopal Church in the U.S.A., it is only part of the Old Catholic Union of Utrecht which remains in 'full communion' with the Churches of the Anglican Communion. Whatever the exact degree of communion between them, such jurisdictions have recognized each other as possessing true bishops ordaining true ministers of word and sacrament. Such cannot be said for some of the proposals for parallel episcopates, which seem to amount to institutional schism by the creation and transfer of parishes in which the diocesan bishop is not recognized. Therefore, we do not recommend the establishment of parallel jurisdiction within the Provinces of the Anglican Communion as an appropriate pastoral solution to this question.

41. A rather different proposal for 'Episcopal Visitors'

has emerged within the discussions between those who remain within the Episcopal Church of the USA (While opposing the ordination of women) and the main body of the Church, which accepts and endorses its official policy as represented by the General Convention. By Resolution B022 of the General Convention, 1988:

1. The Presiding Bishop may designate members of the House of Bishops to act as Episcopal Visitors to provide episcopal sacramental acts for congregations of this Church upon the request and under the authority and direction of the Ecclesiastical Authority of a Diocese. Nothing in this provision shall be construed as abrogating the jurisdiction of the Bishop, or Article II, Section 3 of the Constitution and the Canonical relationships between the Diocesan Bishop and the Congregation, together with its clergy

2. The Diocesan Bishop shall notify the Presiding Bishop's office in writing of all requests and arrangements made in each case. The Presiding Bishop shall make a report in writing to each meeting of the House of Bishops.

3. This provision is only to be used for the transition and incorporation of women into all ordained ministries and is not otherwise applicable.

4. This provision shall remain in effect until, the 71st General Convention and, unless re-affirmed, it shall expire upon its adjournment.

This proposal has, however, met with opposition on both sides. Those who oppose the ordination of women want a mandatory rather than voluntary system. Some of those bishops in favour of women in the priesthood and the episcopate have said they will not consent to an episcopal visitor in their diocese.

42. From an ecclesiological perspective such a scheme can be defended, as a necessary and strictly extraordin-

ary anomaly in preference to schism, if certain conditions are met. Dissenting priests and congregations
must, for their part, not go as far as to refuse canonical
recognition to their diocesan bishop or to say they are
not in communion with their ordinary. This would
mean that their position would have to fall short of
maintaining that the Church could never admit women
to the priesthood or episcopate. But their position could
be expressed as a legitimate hesitancy to affirm the
ordination of women to the priesthood and episcopate
while the matter is in debate in a continuing open
process of reception within the Anglican Communion
and the universal Church. Bishops and dioceses who
accept and endorse the ordination of women to the
priesthood and episcopate would need to recognize, that
within a genuinely open process of reception, there
must still be room for those who disagree. Such bishops
and dioceses would need to understand the problem of
the uncertainty about a eucharist presided over by a
woman and about ordinations by a woman bishop.
Through this sympathetic understanding, bishops and
dioceses would be open to providing a pastoral alternative for those who dissent. Such conditions, on both
sides, would effectively embody the courtesy, respect
and differences of principles spoken of by the Lambeth
Conference. Understood in this way, we recommend
such a proposal be further explored by Provinces in
which there is serious dissent.

43. In our discussion about the nature of communion, it
is clear that a juridical notion of simply being 'in
communion' or 'out of communion' with another
church has been shown to be insufficient. In our
discussions with other churches within the ecumenical
movement we are learning that a real communion has
never been entirely destroyed, even though this cannot
yet be expressed in the shared eucharist which gives
visible sacramental expression to communion. This has

been officially recognized between the Roman Catholic Church and the Orthodox. This is also a common understanding amongst other churches which allow mutual eucharistic hospitality as the appropriate expression of partial communion. A real degree of authentic communion is entailed from the common recognition of baptism among separated churches. It follows that no Province or individual bishop, still less priest or lay person, can meaningfully declare themselves to be categorically out of communion with another Province or bishop.

44. At the same time, integrity prompts the recognition that, at the level of ecclesial communion, which has always included the mutual recognition and interchangeability of ministries, there is an actual diminshment of the degree of communion amongst the provinces of the Anglican Communion. The Lambeth Conference terminology of 'impairment' may be used or other language such as 'restricted' or 'incomplete communion' may be preferred. In either case, communion is less full than it was.

45. Some Provinces have reported that they cannot canonically recognize a woman bishop, or those, male or female, ordained by her, without thereby passing a judgement upon the spiritual fruitfulness of such ministry or using terms such as 'invalid'. Other Provinces have indicated they would regard the orders of a woman bishop as invalid. Yet others have contented themselves with saying that they could not yet move to such a development in their Province but recognize it as right for others. Some Provinces, especially those which already ordain women to the priesthood, have welcomed the admission of women to the episcopate and have implied that they too are likely to do so in the foreseeable future.

46. But recognition that, at the level of the interchangeability of ministries, we have a lesser degree of

communion must not tempt Anglicans into dispensing with the conviction that we are a communion. Talk of an 'Anglican Federation' on the grounds that ministry is not fully interchangeable is not consistent with our understanding of *koinonia*.

47. An excessive concentration on the ordained ministry can mislead us into thinking that communion is only to be defined in terms of the interchangeability of ministries. Lay people will still be free to receive the Holy Communion in Provinces of different principles and practice; and this as of right rather than by ecumenical hospitality. Further, the clergy and bishops of Provinces which differ will still themselves be free to receive Holy Communion together. This illustrates the fact that we are still in communion.

48. If Anglicans mean what they say by an 'open process of reception', such ambiguities will be accepted as one of the growing pains of living in a church where there are no binding central decision making structures. Many Anglicans will actually rejoice in this until there is a more balanced and acceptable model of universal primacy and conciliarity available ecumenically. In any case that is how Anglicanism actually is and has been since wider communion and structures were severed in the 16th century. The first Lambeth Conference called for higher synods above the provincial level precisely for the maintenance of 'Unity in faith and Discipline' (1867, Res 4). But, while this remains an aspiration, we have to live as we actually are a communion still learning what it means to become more fully a communion.

49. In considering ways of maintaining the highest possible degree of communion, regard should be paid not only to theoretical ecclesiology but also to how the Church has lived with less than perfect communion throughout the ages. There have always been anomalies. And yet the Church remains the Church, both

sinful, falling short of what God intends, and yet at the same time the spotless bride of Christ.

50. Ecumenical history furnishes the Anglican Communion with a partial parallel to the problem of the non interchangeability of ministries. When the Church of South India came into being as a united Church in 1947 a significant number of the Provinces of the Communion could not recognize all its presbyters (those who had not been ordained by bishops). They nevertheless remained in the highest degree of communion possible. This parallel does not however correspond exactly. That was a diminishing problem because all the bishops were recognized, and thus all future ordinations. One of the serious dangers of the present situation is the possible emergence of two increasingly separate 'streams' of Anglican ordinations. The Church of South India does, nevertheless, offer an example of an anomaly accepted for the sake of unity.

51. Both protagonists and antagonists of the ordination of women to the priesthood and episcopate should consider carefully what anomalies they are prepared to accept for the sake of unity. Both sides would have to acknowledge that the other's position might, in the long run, prove to be the mind of the Church. It is, for example, possible that in the centuries to come Rome and Orthodoxy would join the consensus in favour. Equally, women's ordination may come to be rejected.

52. For opponents of women's ordination this would mean respect and courtesy for all those whom the Church has ordained to a ministry of word and sacrament by prayer and the laying on of hands, female as well as male. For supporters it would mean respect and courtesy for those who dissent by the toleration of the institutional means for their continuance in the Church and a practice which would ensure the maximum recognition for those ordained by a woman bishop.

53. Acceptance of anomaly is not the compromise of truth. It is to take seriously the imperative to maintain the unity of the Church. When St Paul is faced with dissension in a matter of faith and discipline in the Church of Corinth, his practical solution is to exhort the Corinthians to avoid doing anything offensive to anyone out of consideration for the scruples of others (I Cor. 10:23-33). In a dispute equally concerning faith and conduct St Cyprian similarly writes that he:

> ... considers that in the event of disagreement no compulsion should be brought to bear upon the dissident bishop or bishops. The Church, while still preserving unity, will be obliged to live for a time with the fact of disagreement. (Letter 55)

The *Report of the Archbishop of Canterbury's Commission on Communion and Women in the Episcopate* is copyright.   The Secretary General of the Anglican Consultative Council, 1989.

BIBLIOGRAPHY

This Bibliography is divided into Primary and Secondary Sources. Primary Sources are those that are referred to within the Text of articles, or which are essential background to the articles. Secondary Sources are those Books and articles which have framed the authors' thoughts in a less direct way, or which they consider are worthy of study by those attempting a thorough examination of this issue. There has been no attempt in the bibliography to allot primary or secondary sources to a particular article. This was due to the considerable overlap of source materials between the various contributions.

Primary Sources

Baker, J.A.
'Eucharistic Presidency and Women's Ordination', *Theology 88* 1985
Brown, R.
Crises Facing the Church Paulist Press New York 1975
Burleigh, J.H.S.
A Church History of Scotland Oxford 1960
Calvin, John
Commentary on 1 Corinthians Ed. by D.W. and T.F. Torrance, Eerdmans 1960
Chapman, J.
The Last Bastion Methuen 1989
Cunningham, A.

Christian Women in Ecclesiastical Ministry Seabury New York 1977
de Beauvoir, S.
The Second Sex Alfred Knopf New York 1952
Duncan, Edith
High Albania Virago Press
Fessio, J.
'Admissions of Women to Service at the Altar as Acolytes and Lectors', *The Church Women and Men* Ignatius Press San Francisco 1985
Foh, Susan T.
Woman and the Word of God: A Response to Biblical Feminism Presbyterian and Reformed 1979
Galot, J.
The Theology of the Priesthood Ignatius Press San Francisco 1985
Gray, G.B.
Sacrifice in the Old Testament Oxford 1925
Hauke, M.
Women in the Priesthood: A Systematic Analysis in the light of the Order of Creation and Redemption Ignatius Press San Francisco 1986
Hendriksen, W.
Commentary on Ephesians Banner of Truth 1972
Holloway, E.
'Catholicism, A New Synthesis', *Faith Keyway* 1976
'Thoughts about the Apostolic Letter "Dignity of Womanhood"' *Faith* 21/1 1989
'Sexual Order and Holy Order' *Faith Keyway* 1975
Kenny, M.
Why Christianity Works Michael Joseph 1981
Kirtz, Irma
Malespeak Jonathan Cape 1986
Kung, H.
Why Priests? Collins Glasgow 1972
Macdonald, D.F.
Practice and Procedure in the Church of Scotland 6th

Edition, Church of Scotland 1976
McGowan, A.T.(ed.)
Women Elders in the Kirk? Christian Focus Publications 1990
Moll, H. (ed.)
The Church and Women Ignatius Press 1988
Moore, K.
She for God Alison and Busby 1978
Murray, John
Office in the Church: Collected Writings of John Murray Banner of Truth 1977 Vol 2 pp.357-365
Oddie, W.
What Will Happen to God? Ignatius Press 1988
Quispel, G.
Gnosis als Weltreligion Zurich 1951
Riencourt, A.
Women and Power in History Honeyglen Publishing 1979
Roper, A.
Ist Gott ein Mann? Dusseldorf 1979
Schillebeeckx, E.
Ministry: A Case for Change SCM London 1981
Spong, John
Living in Sin Harper & Row 1989
Stone, L.
The Family, Sex and Marriage in England 1500-1800 Penguin Books 1980
Warner, M.
Alone of All Her Sex Weidenfeld 1976

Secondary Sources

Bailey, S.
'Women and the Churches' Lay Ministry', *Theology* 57 1954 pp.322-30

Baker, J.A.
'The Right Time', *Feminine in the Church* ed. Monica Furlong, London 1984

Barnhouse, R.T.
'Is Patriarchy Obsolete?', *Male and Female* ed. Barnhouse and Holmes, New York 1976

Barr, J.
'The Image of God in the Book of Genesis-A Study of terminology', *BJRL* 51 1968 pp.11-26

Barth, Karl
Church Dogmatics 3, 4 T. & T. Clark 1961

Beckwith, R.T.
Why Not? Priesthood and the Ministry of Women Abingdon 1976

Bedale, S.
'The Meaning of *kephale* in the Pauline Epistles', *JTS* 5 1954 pp.211-15

Berydyaev, N.
The Destiny of Man London 1937

Bilezikian, G.
Beyond Sex Roles Eerdmans Grand Rapids 1985

Bird, P.
'Images of Women in the Old Testament', *Religion and Sexism* ed. R.R. Ruether, New York 1974

Blomfield, F.C.
Wonderful Order London 1955

Boldrey, R. & Boldrey, J.
Chauvinist or Feminist: Paul's View of Women Eerdmans Grand Rapids 1976

Bonhoeffer, D.
Creation and Fall London 1959

Bonner, D.
'Church Law and the Prohibition to Ordain Women', *Women and Priesthood: Future Directions* ed. C. Stuhlmueller, Minnesota 1978

Boucher, M.
'Some Unexplored Parallels to 1 Corinthians 11:11-12 and Galatians 3:28: The New Testament in the Role of Women', *CBQ* 31 1969

Bouyer, L.
Woman and Man with God London 1960

Brandon, S.G.F.
'In the Beginning: the Hebrew Story of the Creation in its Contemporary Setting', *HT* 11 1961 pp.380-7

Bratsiotis, N.P.
'Ish, Ishah', *TDOT* pp.222-35

Briffault, R.S.
The Mothers: A Study of the Origins of Sentiments and Institutions London 1927

Bright, J.
The Authority of the Old Testament London 1967

Brighton, L.A.
'The Ordination of Women: A Twentieth Century Gnostic Heresy?', *Concordia* 8 p.16ff 1982

Brockett, L.
'The Ordination of Women: A Roman Catholic Viewpoint', *MOW Occasional Paper No 4* London 1980

Brooks, B.A.
'Fertility Cult Functionaries in the Old Testament', *JBL* 60 1941 pp.227-53

Brown, E.F.
The Pastoral Epistles London 1917

Brown, R.E.
Biblical Reflections on Crises Facing the Church London 1975
'Roles of Women in the Fourth Gospel', *TS* 36 1975 pp.688-99

Bullough, Vern
The Subordinate Sex: A History of Attitudes Toward Women Urbana, University of Illinois 1973
Burrows, M.
The Basis of Israelite Marriage Abingdon 1976
Caird, G.B.
'Paul and Women's Liberty', *BJRL* 54 1971-2
Principalities and Powers: A Study in Pauline Theology Oxford 1956
Cairns, D.
The Image of God and Man Revised Edition London 1973
Callahan, S.
'Misunderstanding of Sexuality and Resistance to Women Priests', *Women Priests* L. & A. Swidler New York 1977
Carey, G.
I Believe in Man London 1977
Clark, E.
Women and Religion: A Feminist Sourcebook of Christian Thought Harper & Row San Francisco 1977
Clark, S.B.
Man and Woman in Christ Michigan 1980
Coriden, James
Sexism and Church Law Paulist Press New York 1977
Culver, E.T.
Women in the World of Religion New York 1967
Cunningham, A.
'Ecclesial Ministry for Women', in *Future Forms for the Ministry* R. McCormick & G. Dyer 1971
Cupitt, D.
Radicals and the Future of the Church SCM 1989
Daly, M.
Beyond God the Father: Towards a Philosophy of Women's Liberation Boston 1973
The Church and the Second Sex London 1968
Davies, D.
An Anthropological Perspective Abingdon 1976

Dowell, S. & Hurcombe, L.
Dispossessed Daughters of Eve London 1981
Eliade, M.
Patterns in Comparative Religion London 1958
Eller, V.
The Language of Canaan and the Grammar of Feminism Eerdmans Grand Rapids 1982
Epstein, L.M.
Sex Laws and Customs in Judaism New York 1948
Evans, M.
Women in the Bible Exeter 1983
Fiorenza, E.S.
In Memory of Her Crossroads New York 1983
Foh, Susan
Furnish, V.P.
The Moral Teaching of Paul Abingdon, Nashville 1979
Grant, R.M.
Gnosticism and Early Christianity London 1966
Gryson, R.
The Ministry of Women in the Early Church Liturgical Press Minnesota 1976
Hanson, R.
Christian Priesthood Examined Guildford 1979
Harvey, A.E.
Priest or President London 1975
Haughton, R.
The Re-creation of Eve Templegate 1985
Hebblethwaite, M.
Motherhood and God Geoffrey Chapman 1984
Hebblethwaite, P.
'Women Priests?', *Tablet* 229 July 12 1975
Hodgson, L.
'Theological Objections to the Ordination of Women', *Expository Times* 77 1965-6 pp.210-13
Holmes, U.T. & Barnhouse, R. (eds.)
Male and Female New York 1976

Hopko, Thomas (ed.)
Women and the Priesthood St Vladimir's Press Crestwood
NY 1983
James, E.O.
The Cult of the Mother-Goddess London 1959
Jewett, P.K.
Man as Male and Female Eerdmans Grand Rapids 1975
Ordination of Women- Eerdmans Grand Rapids *1980*
Kung, Hans (ed.)
Apostolic Succession: Rethinking a Barrier to Unity Paulist
     Press New York 1968
Keefe, Donald J. "Sacramental Sexuality and the
Ordination of Women" *Communio* (Fall 1978)
Lampe, G.W.H.
'Women and Ministry in the Priesthood' *Explorations in
     Theology 8* London 1981
Macquarrie, J.
Principles of Christian Theology, Revised, London 1977
MacHaffie, B.
Her Story: Women in Christian Tradition Fortress Press
     Philadelphia 1986
Micks, H.M. & Price, C.P. (eds.)
*Toward a New Theology of Ordination: Essays on the
     Ordination of Women* Virginia 1976
Moberly, E.R.
Homosexuality a New Christian Ethic Cambridge 1983
Moltmann-Wendel, E.
*The Women Around Jesus: Reflections on Authentic Person-
     hood* Crossroads New York 1982
Montefiore, H.
Yes to Women Priests Mayhew McCrimmon 1978
Moore, P. (ed.)
Man, Woman and Priesthood SPCK 1978
Ong, Walter J.
Fighting for Life: Contest, Sexuality and Consciousness
Cornell University Press 1981

Otwell, J.H.
And Sarah Laughed: The Status of Women in the Old Testament Philadelphia 1977
Patai, R.
The Hebrew Goddess New York 1967
Pomeroy, Susan
Goddesses, Whores, Wives and Slaves: Women in Classical Antiquity Schocken New York 1975
Proctor, P.
Women in the Pulpit: Is God an Equal Opportunity Employer? Doubleday New York 1976
Rahner, Karl
Concern for the Church: Theological Investigations 20 London 1981
Ruether, R.R.
Religion and Sexism New York 1974
Sexism and God Talk SCM London 1983
Womanguide: Readings Towards a Feminist Theology Beacon Boston 1985
Disputed Questions Orbis Books New York 1989
Russell, Letty
Feminist Interpretation of the Bible Blackwells Oxford 1985
Sanders, E.P.
Jesus and Judaism SCM London
Paul and Palestinian Judaism SCM London
Sapp, S.
Sexuality, the Bible and Science Philadelphia 1977
Saward, J.
Christ and his Bible London 1977
Sayers, Dorothy
Are Women Human? Eerdmans Grand Rapids 1971
Schaffran, J. & Kozak, P.
More than Words: Prayer and Ritual for Inclusive Communities Meyerstone 1988
Schaupp, Joan

Woman, Image of the Holy Spirit Dimension New York 1975

Schillebeeckx, E.
Ministry-A Case for Change London 1981

Scroggs, R.
The Last Adam, A Study in Pauline Anthropology Oxford 1966

Spencer, Aida
Beyond the Curse: Women Called to Ministry Thomas Nelson, Nashville 1985

Stern, Karl
The Flight from Woman Farrar, Straus and Giroux New York 1965

Swidler, L.
Biblical Affirmations of Women Philadelphia 1979

Swidler, L. (ed.) & Swidler, A.
Women Priests: A Catholic Commentary on the Vatican Declaration Paulist Press New York 1977

Tavard, G.H.
Women in Christian Tradition Notre Dame 1973

Tetlow, E.
Women and Ministry in the New Testament Paulist Press New York 1980

Thurian, M.
Priesthood and Ministry London 1983

Tucker, R. & Liefield, W.
Daughters of the Church Zondervan 1987

Vermes, G.
Jesus and the World of Judaism London 1983

WCC Symposium
Concerning the Ordination of Women Geneva 1964

Wijngaards, J.
Did Christ Rule Out Women Priests? Mayhew McCrimmon Great Wakering 1977

Winter, M.T.
Woman Prayer, Woman Song: Resources for Ritual Meyerstone 1987

Index